Contents

GLOSSARY

AECA	Arms Export Control Act
ATCA	Alien Tort Claims Act
BAPSC	British Association of Private Security Companies
CPA	Coalition Provisional Authority, Iraq
DoD	US Department of Defense
EO	Executive Outcomes
ICC	International Criminal Court
ICRC	International Committee of the Red Cross
ID/IQ	Indefinite delivery/infinite quantity
IHL	International humanitarian law
IPOA	International Peace Operations Association
ISS	South African Institute for Security Studies
ITAR	International Traffic in Arms Regulation
KLA	Kosovo Liberation Army
MEJA	Military Extraterritorial Jurisdiction Act
MPRI	Military Professional Resources Incorporated
NBC	National Business Center, US Department of the Interior
NCACC	National Conventional Arms Control Committee
NGOs	Non-governmental organisations
OAU	Organisation for African Unity
PMC	Private military company
PoW	Prisoner of war
PSCs	Private security companies
SIA	Security Industry Authority
UAVs	Unmanned aerial vehicles

INTRODUCTION

Since the late 1990s, the conduct of war and the consequences of its after-math have been transformed. On battlefields, in conflict zones and in areas being rebuilt after war, private actors are playing a progressively more important role. While private companies have often been present on twentieth-century battlefields, notably to provide logistical assistance,[1] their role today is increasingly pivotal. Private companies now provide military and security services ranging from translation to interrogation, from land-mine clearance to close protection for national leaders, and from guarding oil installations to security work for non-governmental organisa-tions (NGOs). Taken together, private security companies (PSCs) provided the second-largest contingent in the US-led 'coalition of the willing' during and after the invasion of Iraq in 2003. There are currently at least 20,000 PSC employees working in Iraq. The scale of private involvement on today's battlefields has not been seen since mercenaries disappeared from state armies in the nineteenth century.[2]

Explosive growth in the private security industry has not been matched by a corresponding development of robust and effective regula-tion. Indeed, many who study the industry point out that PSCs exist in a regulatory vacuum.[3] The absence of effective regulation for an industry that works in war zones, has the capacity to use lethal force and makes a significant contribution to the war efforts of many states is dangerous. Without regulation, the number of companies providing potentially lethal services could grow unchecked, and there are no enforceable rules about who companies can work for and the kinds of work they can do. The laws of war are designed primarily to deal with state actors, and domestic regulations have not caught up with the size of the industry and the nature of the services it offers. Peter Singer, of the Brookings Institution, argues that 'to put it bluntly, the cheese industry is better regulated than the private military industry'.[4] This ought to be a significant concern for the public, state militaries, policymakers and PSCs themselves.

The paucity of effective and overarching regulation means that PSC employees are significantly less accountable for their actions than regular military service personnel. There have been numerous instances when crimes committed by contractors have gone unpunished because of the absence of legal mechanisms of the type that exist in relation to regular military personnel.

In Bosnia in the late 1990s, DynCorp faced a scandal in which some of its employees were engaged in a prostitution ring.[5] The only disciplinary measure taken was to dismiss the employees involved. A loophole in United States legislation meant that the contractors were never called to account for their actions.[6] Private security company employees, often called 'contractors', were embroiled in the prisoner abuse scandal at Abu Ghraib prison in Iraq in 2004. The absence of effective regulation influenced every stage of the scandal. Employees of PSCs were not necessarily trained to do the tasks for which they were hired and were not subject to background checks. The PSCs CACI and Titan provided military interrogators for the prison, 35% of whom lacked formal military training.[7] After the scandal broke, the US military legal machine rolled into action, with formal investigations and courts martial for the military personnel involved. But there were simply no mechanisms to deal with the contractors, not one of whom has been prosecuted to date.

Singer has pointed out that it would be extraordinary if the reason there have been no prosecutions for crimes committed by contractors in Iraq is that they have not committed any crimes. He argues that Westport, Connecticut, with a population of 20,000, has 28 crimes per 100 citizens annually; in Iraq (not known for being as orderly as Westport) none of the 20,000 contractors has been charged with a crime.[8] The absence of prosecutions reflects an absence of regulation.

The relationship between PSCs and non-state actors in post-conflict security environments is even more unregulated than the use of PSCs by states. A state rebuilding after conflict is unlikely to have a robust justice system, from the policing capacity to investigate and arrest to the judicial capacity to try and convict. The 'host state' where foreign militaries and private companies operate is thus not able to control these companies itself. The only sort of enforceable laws are those of the intervening state and international law. In Iraq and Afghanistan, private contractors were specifically immunised against local prosecution, so that even if the host state had the capacity to prosecute, it could not. When a state hires a PSC, the relationship between the state and the company means that the state can (if it chooses, of course) deal with any problems caused by the PSC itself. However, when a PSC is contracted by another private company, such as a natural-resource extraction company, that relationship lacks regulation. The domestic legal system of the host state is not robust enough to enforce criminal laws or indeed the contractual laws governing the PSC–private company relationship. When a state employs a private company, it can bring its laws to bear over the conduct of that company (although this happens less often than it should).

Describing the absence of effective regulation for the private security industry as a vacuum is slightly misleading. Various domestic and international legal instruments may apply. However, even when these legal instruments are specifically intended to deal with today's private security industry – and many of them are not – they are often poorly designed. None of the international legal instruments clearly or directly apply to PSCs, but it is possible to see how they might be or to make a case that they should. The net result is not necessarily a vacuum, but more like a web or patchwork with no overarching and effective regulation. The regulatory web that exists in relation to PSCs includes strands with the potential to catch a rogue PSC or to stop a problem, but also multiple gaps through which it is possible for a PSC to escape.

PSCs themselves are keen to fill the gaps in this regulatory web. Indeed, at least two organisations representing PSCs are staunch advocates of further regulation.[9] PSCs recognise that regulation is good for business. Moreover, many of the lacunae in the regulatory environment directly threaten PSCs and their employees. For example, it is unclear whether PSC employees will be treated as lawful combatants on the battlefield.[10] It is firmly within the interests of PSCs to close these loopholes.

In some cases, PSCs are more enthusiastic about developing regulation, or making regulation more robust, than state governments. In the UK, the government began investigating the possibility of regulating the industry in 2002,[11] but no legislation has been forthcoming. PSCs can and do pose many potential problems, both domestically and internationally. However, it is vital to remember that these problems exist because state governments hire PSCs without regulating them. Thus, if there are problems in the industry, governments bear much of the responsibility.

This paper examines the current regulations that might apply to PSCs before arguing that the development of more effective and more specific regulation, both domestically and internationally, should be a priority for governments. It outlines the nature and role of the private security industry, explaining some other manifestations of private force, identifies five reasons why regulation is necessary, traces the current applicable regulations and discusses their deficiencies. It examines existing domestic regulations, focusing on the United States, South Africa and the United Kingdom, as well as the international legal instruments that might apply to the private security industry. The paper discusses 'informal' regulation, or regulation that does not require the creation of specific laws about PSCs, and how future regulation might be developed to fill in the gaps in the existing regulatory web.

CHAPTER ONE

An Overview of the Industry and the Need for Regulation

The private security industry is complex: it performs a variety of tasks for a wide range of clients in war zones, in peaceful nations and during post-conflict reconstruction. Analysis of the industry has also tended to be complicated, as authors seek to distinguish PSCs from other types of private actor. With as many as 200 companies operating around the world,[1] and working on every continent except Antarctica,[2] an exhaustive analysis of the industry is impossible. There is no attempt here to provide a definitive overview of the industry,[3] the nature and nationality of the companies that compose it,[4] or to discuss in detail where PSCs fit into an overall spectrum of private force.[5] In discussing the challenge of regulation, what is most necessary is to provide an overview of the kinds of contracts PSCs undertake, highlighting some of the difficulties involved in defining what PSCs do, and in differentiating them from other types of actors.

Overview of the industry

PSCs provide four main types of service: logistical support; operational or tactical support; military advice and training; and policing or security. Logistical support entails tasks such as the preparation and delivery of food, laundry and maintenance at military bases. The American company KBR (formerly Kellogg, Brown and Root) is a good example of a logistical support company.[6] These sorts of companies do not pose important regulatory challenges.

PSCs also provide operational or tactical support;[7] this type of support can best be explained as the provision of services normally considered the sole purview of national armed forces (in contrast to logistical support, which has a long history of privatisation). These services may include military interrogation, and even the operation and support of weapons systems. During *Operation Enduring Freedom* in Iraq in 2003, AH-64 *Apache* helicopters and B-2 bombers were supported by contractors,[8] and contractors were used to operate missile guidance systems on US ships, as well as the computer systems for unmanned aerial vehicles (UAVs).[9]

In the 1990s, tactical and operational support included the planning and implementation of combat missions. Executive Outcomes (EO) and Sandline, both now defunct, offered combat services in Sierra Leone, Angola and Papua New Guinea. No PSC operating openly today offers combat services, although in 2006 the American company Blackwater suggested that it would be able to provide a battalion-sized group of peacekeepers for crises like the one in Darfur if authorised by the United Nations.[10]

PSCs also provide security and policing. These services are particularly widespread in Iraq and Afghanistan, where PSCs have provided security for military and political assets, including installations, individuals and convoys.[11] Paul Bremer, head of the Coalition Provisional Authority (CPA) in Iraq, and Afghan President Hamid Karzai have been protected by Blackwater and DynCorp respectively. In some cases PSCs act as police themselves: DynCorp routinely provides the military police that make up American contributions to international missions,[12] including in East Timor and Kosovo. PSCs have also been used to develop and run police and security services. The South Africa-based company Erinys trained, managed and equipped the 16,000-strong Iraq Oil Protection Force.[13] Security services can also be sold to the private sector and to NGOs. In war zones such as Iraq and Afghanistan, virtually all private companies, from the media to telecommunications to extractive industries, require security to do their jobs, and this is usually provided by PSCs.[14] James Cockayne of the International Peace Academy identifies four roles for private security in the NGO and humanitarian sector: guarding installations; providing mobile security escorts; guarding third parties (such as refugee populations); and, less commonly, security analysis and intelligence provision.[15] Deborah Avant of the Elliott School of International Affairs at George Washington University has provided extensive analysis of the use of private security by the World Wildlife Fund.[16]

Providing military advice and training constitutes a significant portion of PSC business. PSCs train armed forces, police forces and auxiliary forces.

The American company Military Professional Resources Incorporated (MPRI) provided training for Croatian forces that was so effective that its protégés had striking success during *Operation Storm*, the offensive to take back Serb-held territory in the Krajina during the summer of 1995. The Croatian victory showed such remarkable operational improvement that MPRI has been dogged by accusations that its personnel must have accompanied their trainees during the mission itself,[17] an accusation that persists despite the absence of evidence. PSCs also provide training as part of post-war reconstruction efforts: DynCorp has trained both the Iraqi and Afghan police forces.

Problems of definition and differentiation

While it is easy to provide an overview of the sort of tasks performed by the private security industry, defining the industry and differentiating it from other private actors is not so simple. First, there are difficulties with assessing the place of PSCs within the spectrum of private force. Second, the placement of PSCs within that spectrum tends to influence the labels used to describe the industry, which vary considerably (and often confusingly).

The role of today's private security industry may be clarified by discussing it in relation to other manifestations of private force, including combat companies like EO and Sandline, modern mercenaries such as those active in Africa in the 1960s and 1970s, and the many pre-twentieth-century manifestations of mercenaries. One way to differentiate actors who use private force is to organise them into categories on the basis of what they do, and for whom they do it. Singer uses a 'tip of the spear' approach, in which he classifies companies on the basis of the lethality of the services they provide, ranging from the lethal combat capacity of companies like EO and Sandline to the relatively non-lethal capacity associated with training and advising.[18] Christopher Kinsey, an academic expert on PSCs, uses a typology that attempts to organise companies into four quadrants on the basis of whether or not they employ lethal force and whether the object they attempt to secure is private (an installation, for example) or public (which he defines as state authority).

There are, however, noticeable difficulties with these sorts of categorisations. As Kinsey notes, it is hard to organise PSCs into tidy categories, because they provide such a wide range of services.[19] Sometimes the same PSC might provide a non-lethal service (such as land-mine clearance), as well as one with significantly greater potential for lethality (such as close protection for an important political figure). The 'lethality' distinction is often made in terms of offensive or defensive capacity, or in terms of whether or not a company engages in active combat or passive defensive action. Most PSCs assert that they will only use force in self-defence and that they do not actively engage in combat.[20] However, the distinction between offense and defence, or combat and non-combat, is also a blunt instrument when used to differentiate between companies. Caroline Holmqvist, of the Stockholm Institute for Peace Research, argues that 'what is perceived as "defensive" under one set of circumstances may well turn out to have "offensive" repercussions in another' and that 'the ability of companies to provide many different services simultaneously makes the 'offensive–defensive' or 'active–passive' distinctions irrelevant at best or misleading at worst'.[21] Advice and training, which are technically neutral and do not constitute actual combat, can nonetheless have a lethal impact as the trainee force becomes more effective.[22] The Blackwater employees providing Paul Bremer's security in Iraq had their own weapons and their own helicopters, and 'fought off insurgents in ways that were hard to distinguish from combat'.[23] Differentiating between actors who use force on the basis of lethality and the nature of the force deployed is clearly challenging.

There are further difficulties with the labels applied to the private security industry. The term 'mercenary' inevitably creeps into discussions about private force, and it has become so pejorative that Avant suggests avoiding it entirely.[24] There is no real question that PSCs and mercenaries differ considerably. PSCs are organised entities with a permanent presence, and are capable of taking on complex and long-term projects. They claim to be discriminating with regard to their clients, and seek to avoid direct combat. Mercenaries, on the other hand, work either individually or in loosely organised groups. They are not particular about their employers and will provide a wide range of services, including engagement in combat. There are also questions about whether or not PSCs can be differentiated from the combat companies of the 1990s, like EO and Sandline. It seems that they can, as no company operating today openly provides the sorts of services (including planning missions and fighting them) that these two companies offered. There are other clear lines of continuity between all three types of actor, however. All three exchange force for financial reward, and PSCs and combat companies differ only in the degree of combat they will provide.

The confusion that results from organising the industry into categories and differentiating it from other types of private force is further compounded by the variety of labels used to describe it. Sometimes the term 'private military company' (PMC) is used; confusingly sometimes authors take the term to include all types of companies, including combat companies, and sometimes PMC is used to refer exclusively to combat companies.[25] PSCs themselves make this latter distinction and avoid the term PMC. Singer opts for a totally different term, PMF, or private military firm.[26]

The question, then, is how to find the way out of the maze of acronyms that refer to the industry and how to differentiate PSCs from other actors. The term PSC is used here to refer to the type of company operating today in Iraq and Afghanistan: companies that provide a wide range of military and security services but avoid combat. This also reflects the terminology used by the industry itself.

Differentiating PSCs from each other and from PMCs may be achieved by focusing on specific contracts rather than on the nature of the actors themselves.[27] Relying on contracts as the tool of differentiation is also useful because it helps to distinguish PSCs from mercenaries: the latter are unlikely to have official or formal contracts, and if they do, they might include combat or even illegal activity, such as organising coups d'état. Contracts explicitly calling for combat services and informal agreements to hire mercenary groups are not examined here, as they pose different sets of problems requiring specific regulation.

The five main reasons for regulation

Better regulation of the private security industry is vital. While domestic, international and informal regulation exists, there is a strong case that the current system is deficient and contains significant gaps. Regulation is necessary for five main reasons: because PSCs challenge both political and military control; because the rules governing PSCs are unclear; because the industry suffers from a lack of transparency; because PSCs are insufficiently accountable for their actions; and because the industry's future growth ought to be monitored to protect the public interest. The problems outlined stem essentially from a lack of state-directed regulation rather than from problems inherent in the nature of PSCs.

Control

The privatisation of military functions, particularly those formerly associated with the state, has a significant impact on the way states control military force. Avant points out that the use of PSCs affects three different types of state control over force: functional (the effectiveness of the military); political (which actors, organisations or individuals control force);

and social (the degree to which the use of force is congruent with broader social values, including democracy, international law, human rights and the protection of civilians in warfare). In addition, the privatisation of security can affect how well these types of control fit together. A good fit holds the 'key to stable, legitimate, and effective civil–military relations – the situation we recognize as effective control'.[28] She concludes that although the privatisation of security has different effects in weak and strong states, and that the type of company hired will also make a difference to the degree of change, all three types of control are transformed by privatisation, as is the way they fit together.[29]

Indeed, it is easy to find examples where privatisation undermines control, particularly political and military control (which Avant defines as functional control). The undermining effects of privatisation on political and military control should prompt two types of regulatory debate: one on how regulation can ameliorate some of these changes, and another on the general advisability of privatising some aspects of state security.

The traditional political controls placed on the use of force change with the privatisation of security. In particular, many of the institutional constraints that surround the decision to send state military forces into action can be circumvented by the use of private force.

In the United States, the privatisation of force affects the mechanics of governmental decisions to use force. The use of PSCs privileges the executive branch over the legislative branch of government; in other words, by using PSCs, the president is able to reduce the role Congress would normally play in decisions about the use of force. When a PSC gets a US government contract for training a foreign military or police service, these decisions are not approved by Congress, and congressional oversight becomes difficult.[30] Sometimes training contracts can have a significant impact upon the outcome of a conflict. In these circumstances, a training contract can become a means to conduct foreign policy without congressional oversight. In Croatia, the US influenced the outcome of the conflict without having to take sides publicly and without congressional debate.

Using contractors may help states to avoid the problem of 'troop ceilings', or the stated number of troops that can be sent to a conflict without triggering a further oversight mechanism or debate. In the US, private contractors can be used to increase troop numbers without surpassing troop ceilings, thereby eliminating congressional oversight.[31] Troop ceilings can also be set by states hosting an international force or by the executive branch itself, and can then be circumvented by using contractors.[32]

The use of contractors may also diminish the role that public opinion plays in reining in a state that has embarked on an unpopular war, or even the decision to go to war in the first place. By using contractors, governments may 'carry out actions that generally would not gain legislative or public approval'.[33] The state has to mobilise fewer of its own troops to fight and recruiting problems may be avoided. There is less media coverage about the deaths of contractors than about the loss of regular soldiers.[34] Avant asserts that in the *New York Times* in 2004, there were 40 articles about regular troops for every one on private security personnel.[35] Sustaining an unpopular war becomes easier if the state's own army is not suffering casualties and the burden of replacing troops is eased by the presence of a large number of contractors.[36] The discussions about military overstretch taking place in 2006 in relation to both the UK and the US would be even more heated in the absence of the 20,000 contractors assisting both states in Iraq.

The problems the private security industry poses for political control are clearly of the state's (rather than the industry's) making. It may well be in the state's interest to reduce these controls on foreign policy. Whether or not it is in the public interest is another question, and a debate about regulation would force some of these concerns into the public domain.

The use of PSCs also has a significant impact on military control over the use of force on the battlefield, and on military capacity more generally. The presence of private contractors on the battlefield can undermine the military chain of command. PSCs add another level of complexity to the military decision-making process; commanders must focus on their own units but also take into consideration the PSCs working near or with them.[37] Unlike regular soldiers, very little prevents contractors from abandoning their duties and leaving the battlefield.[38] During periods of intensified violence in Iraq, the US 'faced a wave of firms delaying, suspending or ending operations because they found it too dangerous, with inevitable resultant stresses' on supplies and on the war.[39] Moreover, the use of contractors prevents the military from dealing with personnel shortages by reassigning troops to different roles. For example, logistical troops can take on front-line battle roles, acting as the 'infantry in reserve'.[40] Privatisation may reduce military flexibility on the battlefield.

Military control over PSCs is sometimes diminished because the military itself is not informed of contractor actions or because of communication problems between the two groups. David Isenberg, of the British American Security Information Council, argues that 'press reports indicate serious confusion in authority between PMCs and the military'.[41] Contractors are not always required to keep the military command informed about their actions, 'leading to absurd situations like in Najaf, in which private contractors fought off attacks on the CPA headquarters that military officials learned of only hours later'.[42] The UK-based PSC Hart was involved in a firefight that required military support; when that support did not arrive it was forced to hold its position for some time.[43] Indeed, some senior military officials have only a limited understanding of the kinds of work that PSCs undertake in the theatre of war. Singer refers to an American four-star general who was not aware that contractors in Iraq were armed.[44] The then US Army Secretary Thomas E. White stated in a memo in 2002, before the war in Iraq, that the army did not have enough information to manage its rapidly growing number of contractors.[45]

A chain of command that only incorporates PSCs inadequately further reduces control over military force, because PSCs and soldiers might not be held to the same standards. There have been incidents where PSC actions might have undermined the goal of a broader mission. As Fred Schreier and Marina Caparini of the Geneva Centre for the Democratic Control of Armed Forces indicate, conflicts such as Iraq require precise calibration of the amount of force used, given the importance of not alienating the local population. However, PSC employees are not subject to military discipline.[46] This means that the mechanisms used to ensure that soldiers do not use force in a way that might undermine the overall strategic goal are not in place to deal with contractors.

Regulation could help to improve these problems of military control through the simple improvement of procedures: contracts could be tightened, and oversight developed further. However, an important question is whether developing elaborate regulation to ensure better coordination and clearer lines of command and control might involve spending time and energy 'reinventing the wheel'. If the military already has effective command and control mechanisms, why not return functions like close protection to the military?

Clarity

A wider absence of clarity, not just in terms of command and control, is a routine problem in the private security industry. One of the main reasons that regulation is necessary is because it has the potential to clear up many confused or complicated issues, making the battlefield safer for contractors, civilians and regular soldiers, and at the same time differentiating legitimate PSCs from some of their illegitimate competitors.

Opaque rules raise two issues for regulation. First, there is the vexed question of the status of contractors on the battlefield. Second, there is a lack of clarity within the industry itself, as there are illegitimate as well as legitimate players, employees who sometimes move from the former to the latter, and vice versa, compounding regulatory problems.

Clarifying the status of contractors in theatres of war would be of great benefit to all contractors and their employers, and would undoubtedly go a long way towards reducing confusion on the battlefield. The grey areas between combat and non-combat, and offensive and defensive action, outlined above, cause difficulties for contractors. It is unclear, according to the rules of international humanitarian law, whether or not a contractor on the battlefield is a civilian, a lawful combatant or an unlawful combatant. Situations where some individuals perform non-combat functions that nonetheless support a larger military effort, or where contractors might appear to adversaries to be indistinguishable from regular troops, such as in the provision of close protection, complicate matters further. The US Air Force Judge Advocate General has argued that civilian UAV operators risk losing their non-combatant status because they provide crucial combat support. They could, therefore, be considered unlawful combatants.[47] If a person whose combatant status is unclear is captured, it leaves the decision on treatment up to the captor, and might mean a prisoner does not get treated according to the rules set out in the Geneva Conventions.[48]

The question of combatant status might matter more in terms of academic debate than it matters to contractors on the battlefield. On the one hand, an unlawful combatant loses certain prisoner-of-war (PoW) rights and runs the risk of criminal prosecution. On the other, insurgents or terrorists are unlikely to follow the Geneva Conventions in their treatment of prisoners and the International Criminal Court (ICC) has not yet proved to be a particularly robust institution, so the real consequences of being considered an unlawful combatant may be less serious than often argued.

However, providing greater clarity regarding the application of international humanitarian law to contractors would undoubtedly reduce confusion on the battlefield. The laws of war derive from the behaviour and codes of professional military officers in the nineteenth century,[49] codes that were often based on simple practicality and the desire to minimise the negative effects of war. The rules associated with surrender, for example, make war easier to manage, and rules about wearing uniform protect civilians by revealing legitimate targets of war and allowing civilians to see who is potentially dangerous. Clarifying who's who on the battlefield, and sorting out what they are allowed to do, makes war more clear both for participants and for bystanders. It is for this reason that legal or regulatory clarity needs to be applied to PSCs in Iraq.[50]

Regulation could improve clarity in the private security industry in another way. One of the major problems facing PSCs is their desire to differentiate themselves from companies at the less legitimate end of the industry, or from the sorts of groups that plan operations like the 2004 coup attempt in Equatorial Guinea. A strong regulatory regime, however composed, could serve to separate legitimate companies, which abide by international humanitarian law, work closely with their home states, choose their clients carefully and provide a variety of mechanisms to ensure the accountability of their employees, from illegitimate companies or groups that do none of these and are willing to work for any client. Providing this kind of separation is a stated desire of the British Association of Private Security Companies (BAPSC) and its members.[51] Joining an industry organisation, like the BAPSC or the International Peace Operations Association (IPOA), and abiding by domestic or international regulations will quickly reveal the companies that want to be regarded as legitimate purveyors of security on the international stage.

However, another area suffering from a lack of clarity might complicate the separating function of regulation. One of the reasons it is hard to characterise the private security industry is that its personnel are often or have in the past been employed by combat companies and mercenary groups. There are no clear rules about who PSCs can hire and no clear way to distinguish good employees from bad employees. Private security companies function without a large permanent staff and recruit employees from a database for specific tasks. At the moment, there are no binding guidelines for the vetting of personnel. There is nothing to stop an individual from working for a perfectly legitimate PSC one day and for a dubious mercenary operation the next. Andrew Bearpark, Director General of the BAPSC, recounts watching television one night and discovering that the PSC employees who had provided his security in Iraq were under arrest for their participation in the Equatorial Guinea coup.[52] The company MPRI has struggled to deal with accusations that it trained the Kosovo Liberation Army (KLA), which it denies; however, former MPRI employees have done freelance consulting for the KLA.[53] Companies themselves can compound this problem by making poor recruitment decisions. The rapid growth of the industry since the invasion of Iraq in 2003 has led companies to recruit less desirable employees. Blackwater, for example, reportedly hired former Chilean officers who had served under Augusto Pinochet.[54]

More effective regulation could reduce the problems caused by unclear recruiting practices and blurred lines between the legitimate and the illegitimate ends of the industry. As Singer puts it, there are 'insufficient controls over who can work for these firms and who these firms can work for'.[55] Regulation requiring background checks is one option, and the creation of a blacklist containing the names of employees who have committed abuses or have worked as mercenaries is another.

Transparency

Today's private security industry is notably lacking in transparency, a situation that could be improved by more effective regulation. Simple facts about the industry are difficult and sometimes impossible to come by, and others are obscured because of the way that states make contracts with PSCs. The industry's size, the economic savings (if any) of using private force, the number of contractor deaths, and the contracts themselves are far less transparent than they should be. A lack of information about the industry prevents effective public oversight and diminishes the capacity to make good decisions about the use of private force. Regulation, or even a debate about regulation, might force more openness about some of these issues.

Estimates of the size of the private security industry vary hugely, meaning that some of the basic facts necessary for regulation are unavailable. The most common estimate of the number of contractors in Iraq is 20,000, working for as many as 60 firms.[56] But the actual number could be far larger.[57] It is difficult, if not impossible, to estimate the number of contractors working in Afghanistan, and both sets of numbers are compounded by the growth of indigenous PSCs hiring local staff providing security to private organisations. These companies are unlikely to be counted in official totals. More stringent regulation would help to reveal the number of companies and employees operating around the world, allowing a higher degree of public oversight and opening a debate as to whether widespread privatisation is advisable. It is surprising, and ought to be unacceptable for governments and the public, that an industry with the power to affect the course of conflict around the world is so difficult to quantify.

If the industry's true size is murky and difficult to discover, then hard facts about its cost are even more opaque. One of the frequent claims about military privatisation is that it saves governments and taxpayers money. PSCs do not have to provide the same support to their employees as national militaries do, and not paying for the provision of food, training and hospitals should make contractors cheaper than soldiers.[58] Moreover, the state need not pay for the training of contractors. A general view that privatisation is better and cheaper for states influences the view that using PSCs will save governments money.[59]

However, it is by no means clear that PSCs reduce the cost of war. This is partly because confirmed figures about cost are not available, partly because the industry suffers from inadequate competition, which distorts the cost of its activities,[60] and partly because hiring a PSC might really be a false economy. It is not necessarily true that contractors are cheaper than regular soldiers,[61] though it is impossible to say for certain because of the absence of evidence about the industry's real cost. The Center for Public Integrity, a Washington-based organisation promoting investigative journalism in the public interest, asserts that US companies have received up to US$48.7 billion for work in Afghanistan and Iraq; in 2006, *Business Week* estimated that the US had spent $104bn on contract security services (excluding weapons and research and development).[62]

The private security industry is characterised by inadequacies in the competition for contracts and the structure of contract administration, leading to a situation where governments may end up spending more than they save.[63] Singer argues that the US government in Iraq not only failed to 'make an attempt to see if contracting would save it money, but instead set up structures that almost ensured that it would not'.[64] International law scholar Laura Dickinson is more forthright still, asserting that 'corruption and fraud have been rampant in the Iraqi contracts'.[65]

Finally, in contracting out to the private sector, the appearance of economising by using PSCs may be deceptive. The fact that the government need not pay for training is not necessarily a saving, given that many contractors are retired state soldiers, trained at state expense. In the case of the UK, the number of soldiers leaving the armed forces and joining the private sector is so large that mechanisms to encourage soldiers to stay enlisted, such as offering year-long 'sabbaticals', have been necessary.[66] The private security industry 'uses public funds to provide higher pay and then charges back the military at a higher rate, all for the human capital investment that the public institution originally paid for'.[67]

Just as the industry's size and cost are far less transparent than they should be, so too are the number of contractor deaths, which may help to disguise the true human cost of war. Every time battle deaths in Iraq reach new thresholds, sombre news reports discuss the significance of the first 100, 500 and 1,000 deaths, and so on. However, contractor deaths are excluded from these totals. By August 2006, 608 contractors had been killed in Iraq.[68] The 2,000[th] casualty in Iraq came much earlier than October 2005 when it was reported in the media.[69] Regulation could specifically require the public reporting of contractor deaths, or a debate about regulation could help to bring contractor losses under greater scrutiny.

Finally, the contracts used in the industry are themselves difficult to find. This makes it difficult to tell whether they are effectively governing contractor behaviour, or if billing practices are problematic, or the number of individuals hired under each contract.[70] It is not possible to make a Freedom of Information request for PSC contracts in the United States, as the information is considered both proprietary and associated with national security.[71] Regulation could require that these contracts be made publicly available.

Accountability

Perhaps the most important reason to regulate the private security industry is to ensure that PSC contractors are held accountable for their actions, at least to the same standard as regular soldiers. As the problems with civilian shootings, the scandal at Abu Ghraib and the DynCorp prostitution scandal demonstrate, insufficient legal accountability remains a significant problem for the industry. There are too few effective and applicable instruments for prosecuting contractors. The main mechanism for ensuring that employees are not only thoroughly vetted but held to account is the goodwill of PSCs themselves. Some companies do work hard to ensure that when problems occur, they provide all available assistance to resolve them. However, relying on the continued good behaviour of PSCs in an arena this sensitive is simply not good enough to ensure public safety.

Future growth of the industry[72]

A final reason to regulate the industry is to shape its future growth. While the Iraq 'bubble' of financial windfall may have burst,[73] and such extensive privatisation may not happen again, the private security industry is not going to disappear. This is perhaps the most compelling reason for regulation. States and their citizens need to decide how much privatisation is too much, and to set boundaries about which functions should be privatised and which should not. Without this sort of regulation, the industry will simply evolve unchecked and unmonitored. States could and should use regulation to direct this growth.

Conclusion

More effective regulation will help states and militaries to enhance their control over the private security industry. It will assist in bringing greater clarity to PSC operations; it will make the industry more transparent; and it will ensure that there are more effective and better developed mechanisms to call PSCs to account for their actions. Perhaps most importantly, regulation will set down rules for the industry's future growth. If the private security industry is here to stay, then it is necessary for governments to ensure that they control it, and to direct its future growth. The public, both in the states from which PSCs operate and in the states that use PSCs alongside their armed forces, has been notably left out of the debate on privatisation. In part, the absence of public debate has stemmed from the ability of governments to use PSCs in order to avoid scrutiny (as is the case with manipulating threshold levels). Public participation is made more difficult by the lack of transparency associated with the industry. Effective regulation can make PSCs a useful part of a government's military arsenal, while ensuring that the public is kept informed about an important shift in the way governments prepare for and fight wars.

CHAPTER TWO

Domestic Regulation

Regulations created by states to deal with PSCs operating within their territory form part of the web currently controlling the private security industry. Domestic regulation succeeds in some arenas. It seems obvious that when states contract PSCs to assist with state-approved projects or to work alongside government armed forces the state itself should decide on the rules governing the relationship. However, domestic regulation on its own is incapable of solving all the problems that have been outlined so far. Relying solely on domestic regulation to control PSCs leaves regulatory gaps open. The most serious of these problems is the fact that if regulations in one state are too tight, PSCs may simply move to states with weaker rules. Indeed, states take vastly different regulatory approaches. The focus here is on three national domestic regulatory systems – those of the United States, the United Kingdom and South Africa – and the strong and weak points of each system. The general deficiencies of domestic regulation and the problems of a wholly domestic approach to regulating the private security industry are also discussed.

Domestic regulation in the United States

The current system of PSC regulation in the United States has two components. First, there is a licensing system, whereby potential PSC contracts are scrutinised. Second, there are laws regarding the prosecution of contractors for crimes committed while serving abroad.

The licensing system: International Traffic in Arms Regulation (ITAR) and the Arms Export Control Act (AECA)

The United States uses the same methods to control PSC services as it uses to control the sale of arms and other defence services. In theory, just as the sale of arms is regulated to ensure that it promotes broader American policy, the sale of security services such as those offered by PSCs is scrutinised by specific government bodies. Private security companies' services are dealt with using the ITAR, which is part of the AECA. The ITAR's provisions for the sale of services were adapted to deal with the private security industry,[1] specifically the sale of 'defence services' or the sale of assistance, technical data or training related to military units.[2] The ITAR is administered by the Office of Defense Trade Controls (based in the Department of State).

ITAR is used to grant licences for PSCs to sell their services abroad. Some countries, such as those deemed to be a threat to the United States, are proscribed from buying security services (just as they are prevented from buying US weapons). A PSC application is sent to relevant parties within the State Department for comment: regional desks, the political–military bureau, country specialists and others like the Bureau of Democracy, Human Rights and Trade.[3] Before an application can be approved, it must be checked against the list of proscribed countries; in cases where it is not clear whether or not the client is proscribed, the Assistant Secretary decides after hearing from the parties within the State Department affected by the decision.[4]

There are several specific problems with the ITAR system. First, the licensing process is repeatedly described as idiosyncratic and inconsistent.[5] The offices involved change from contract to contract, and 'neither the companies nor independent observers are exactly clear about how the process works'.[6] Second, Congress is only notified about a contract going through the ITAR process after a threshold of US$50 million has been reached, and contracts can be written specifically so that they fall below this threshold, thus avoiding the licensing process. There is 'nothing to prevent a company from selling several separate contracts for services to avoid the $50m bar'.[7] Third, even if a licence is granted, there are no real oversight mechanisms in place. One option is for the embassy or consulate in the country receiving the services to keep an eye on the contract,[8] which presupposes that they have the time and the inclination to enter battle zones. Many officials believe that oversight is 'contrary to their job'.[9]

Contracts for security services are rarely administered or overseen by officials with the relevant training and expertise.[10] The industry's rapid growth has worsened this problem, as the number of qualified contract administrators in the Pentagon cannot meet the demand. Even before 11 September 2001, there were shortages in the number of administrative personnel, and the growth in the number of contracts awarded subsequently has not been matched by recruitment of administrators; indeed, posts in this area have been cut back.[11] Pressure to fill contracts results in poor administration. The focus is first on 'upon *awarding* contracts and less upon *administering* those contracts once awarded'.[12] On the ground in Iraq, the monitoring of PSC contracts has been provided by a PSC which is itself a major US government contractor.[13] It is hard to imagine this situation occurring in any other industry; automotive safety standards are not and should not be supervised by a car company.

Contracts, furthermore, are not awarded in a manner that encourages competition and accountability. In the United States, complicated budget rules mean that one agency can ask another to award and administer a contract. There is a 'proliferation of fee-based arrangements that permit government agencies to avoid longstanding contracting constraints by offloading their procurement functions to other agencies'.[14] The contractors involved in the scandal at Abu Ghraib, acting as interpreters and interrogators for the US Army, were hired under a contract with the Department of the Interior's National Business Center (NBC). The problem with this system is that the NBC, which was paid a fee to arrange for the award of the contract, had no major incentive to manage it. For a 'nominal fee, the NBC permitted the Army to inappropriately use a streamlined, commercial contracting vehicle to obtain contractor personnel through a closed, non-competitive process, after which neither Army nor Interior procurement personnel' managed contractor performance.[15] A further problem with this type of fee-based contract exchange is that, until 2005, only contractors employed by the Department of Defense itself could be prosecuted under the Military Extraterritorial Jurisdiction Act (MEJA).

Finally, inappropriate contracts are often used for security services. Contracts that fix a price in advance but do not specify either the services to be provided or when they are to be delivered are used frequently. In theory, one overarching contract is put in place and then companies compete to fulfil aspects of it. These 'indefinite delivery/infinite quantity' (ID/IQ) contracts are popular in part because they solve a particular problem with the contractual regulation of PSCs. If a contract is too specific, it may slow down a company's ability to fulfil it and perhaps make it uneconomical to compete for the contract in the first place. ID/IQ contracts ensure that contractors arrive and begin work quickly. Because the contractors are unlimited, companies can easily abuse the system by overcharging for work.[16] Competition for each part of the overarching contract rarely occurs and agencies focused on speed and convenience often hire only one company to fulfil the whole contract.[17]

The licensing and contract scheme used to deal with PSCs in the United States demonstrates how existing legislation intended to regulate the sale of arms can be adapted to control PSCs. However, the US system also demonstrates that oversight is a necessary part of the contracting process; that the kinds of contracts used need to be considered carefully; and that governmental idiosyncrasies, like the contract exchange between agencies, can affect accountability. Problems with oversight in the American system also indicate the hidden cost of privatisation: oversight mechanisms require substantial investments in order to be effective, in particular, large numbers of personnel must be hired to deal with contracts and procurement.

The prosecution system: the Military Extraterritorial Jurisdiction Act

The MEJA was passed in 2000 in order to ensure that non-military personnel associated with the American military abroad could be prosecuted in the United States for crimes in situations where the host nation was unwilling or unable to do so. It was not specifically designed to deal with contractors, but rather to deal with crimes committed by any civilian accompanying or working with the American military, including the spouses of service personnel. However, it was quickly applied to contractors, in part because under Status of Forces Agreements US personnel of all types are often immune to prosecution by local governments. The DynCorp employees who were involved in the prostitution ring scandal in Bosnia avoided prosecution because of this loophole.[18] In Iraq, under CPA Order 17, contractors had immunity from Iraqi prosecution. Immunising contractors from local prosecution is a double-edged sword. On the one hand, it is useful because it protects non-military personnel from being tried in a state with a flawed judicial system or where it would be unlikely that they would receive a fair trial. On the other hand, it has made it impossible to call contractors to account for their actions.

Because the MEJA was not designed specifically to deal with contractors, it has not been a robust way of ensuring that PSC employees can be prosecuted for crimes committed abroad. The MEJA originally only applied to contractors who were working directly for the Department of Defense (DoD) or a contractor hired by the DoD. But the contractors embroiled in the Abu Ghraib scandal were employed by the Department of the Interior, and so could not be prosecuted. This gap was closed by legislation designed to include any contractors working for any federal agency supporting the DoD's missions abroad.[19] However, some agencies, including the Federal Bureau of Investigation, the Drug Enforcement Agency, the Central Intelligence Agency and the Department of Homeland Security, still fall outside this definition.[20] Nor does the MEJA apply to Americans hired by PSCs working for other governments.[21] The Patriot Act of 2001 further tightens these loopholes as it extends to crimes committed by or against Americans on lands or facilities designated for American use.[22] However, the Patriot Act's jurisdiction would not include activities away from US bases or other facilities.

A second problem with the MEJA is that the legislation was designed to include 'implementing regulations' that would have allowed the legislation to work more effectively, and these took years to come into force. When the MEJA was created, it required the Secretary of Defense to prescribe 'regulations governing the apprehension, detention and removal of persons under MEJA' and to make these regulations uniform across all branches of the American armed forces. Without the implementing regulations, it was unclear who could arrest and detain civilian contractors. Neither was it clear how long the US should wait for host countries to begin prosecution, where it was possible for them to do so.[23] Implementing regulations finally came into force in 2006.

The MEJA only applies to crimes punishable by one year or more of imprisonment, effectively excluding 'misdemeanours'.[24] While the effects of excluding misdemeanours from the legislation might appear minimal, in practice it could have an impact both on military discipline and on community relations. Unpunished misdemeanours such as petty theft may alienate local populations and breed resentment among regular soldiers who are called to account for their actions.

Finally, as with all prosecutions, the MEJA relies on the desire of prosecutors to bring a case to court. Extraterritorial prosecutions are complex and expensive, as all the relevant detail about the crime (including witnesses and evidence) are located far away. The absence of prosecutorial will is one explanation for the dearth of prosecutions under the MEJA.

Despite the shortcomings of the MEJA, the basic idea of creating extraterritorial legislation to control contractors is good. In situations where contractors are immunised from local prosecution and not subject to courts martial, the ability to prosecute for contractor crimes would be an essential part of any attempt to regulate PSCs. However, the legislation must be carefully designed. And it is worth noting that even though the MEJA has existed since 2000, and though contractors are widely alleged to have committed crimes in Iraq, as of September 2006 no contractor had been prosecuted under the MEJA.[25] Extraterritorial prosecutions are a tool that might best be described as better than nothing but far from good enough.

However, the American approach is not the only potential model for the domestic regulation of PSCs.

Domestic regulation in South Africa

South Africa approaches the legal control of the private security industry in a completely different manner. Rather than seeking to place controls on the industry, the South African system effectively attempts to ban it. The difference in approach can partly be explained by South Africa's apartheid history and experience with the combat company, EO.

EO came to prominence in the mid-1990s, when it provided security services and 'combat solutions' for Angola and Sierra Leone. It famously and controversially incorporated many members of the South African army's 32 Battalion, notorious for its apartheid-era activities.[26] Its activities garnered significant attention, both positive and negative, but its apartheid links proved to be embarrassing to the post-apartheid government, which 'embarked on a campaign to "leash" the dogs of war'.[27] The Regulation of Foreign Military Assistance Act (1998) differentiates between mercenary activity, which it defines as 'direct participation as a combatant in armed conflict for private gain', and 'foreign military assistance', which is defined as military advice or training short of combat, security services, or any activity which may have the effect of assisting a party to armed conflict or overthrowing the government. The act bans mercenary activity outright, and requires any type of foreign military assistance to be examined by the National Conventional Arms Control Committee (NCACC), which looks at the relationship of the intended recipient to the armed conflict, and provides a licence, which it retains the power to revoke. It applies to all South African citizens and passport holders.[28]

The act suffered from major enforcement problems and until 2003, there were no prosecutions under its auspices. There have since been two prosecutions, a very small number given the large amount of South African PSC activity.[29] The act is often criticised for trying to encompass too many actors and for being imprecise. There is an argument that some of its provisions violate the right of South Africans to choose their own occupations, which is protected in the South African constitution.[30] The act defines what constitutes military assistance very broadly. This broad definition means that it could be applied to many different actors, including actors not normally considered military in nature, such as humanitarian agencies.[31]

South African legislation demonstrates some of the more challenging problems associated with domestic regulatory regimes. Domestic regulation that is too tight will force companies to relocate abroad or to go underground; after the first piece of legislation, EO officially went out of business and apparently reconstituted itself in several new forms.[32] And, if companies go underground, they are harder to reach with legislation.[33] One view is that legislation will only affect legitimate companies seeking to be regulated and make it more difficult for them to conduct business, while opening up opportunities for companies operating at the margins of the industry.[34]

Since 2005 the South African government has been debating the creation of new legislation to deal with the issues caused by private force. The Prohibition of Mercenary Activities and Prohibition and Regulation of Certain Activities in Areas of Armed Conflict Bill passed through the committee stage in late August 2006. It will now have to be passed by both houses and signed into law by the president. The bill has several goals:

> To prohibit mercenary activity; to prohibit, subject to exceptions, the provision of assistance of service of a military, security, or other nature in an area of armed conflict; to prohibit, subject to exceptions, the enlistment of South African citizens or permanent residents in foreign armed forces; to regulate the provision of humanitarian aid in an area of armed conflict; to provide for extraterritorial jurisdiction for the courts of the republic with regard to certain offences.

Individuals and companies must apply to the NCACC before selling any service to an area of armed conflict. Humanitarian services cannot be provided without explicit authorisation.

The bill suffers from important potential shortcomings. One of the most significant is its broad scope. The term 'areas of armed conflict' is particularly vague, and so the new legislation could be used against South Africans working all over the world in a variety of scenarios. To make matters more complex, the bill excludes acts that assist popular struggles for national liberation, self-determination and resistance against foreign occupation. While this measure is understandable, given South Africa's history, it makes deciding whether or not assistance is legal even more complicated.

The foreign enlistment provisions could mean that South Africans are no longer able to serve in the British army, a concern that was brought up by Paul Boateng, the British High Commissioner in South Africa, during the committee phase of the bill. 'Security services' are defined broadly and include some relatively uncontroversial services, like medical and para-medical services and the procurement of equipment. Regulating these services may prevent necessary and legitimate assistance from reaching war-torn countries. The tighter regulations for humanitarian agencies will have the same effect, and it is not clear why they are included in a bill dealing with the provision of security services.

A variety of actors have expressed serious concerns about the bill, including the IPOA and the South African Institute for Security Studies (ISS). Len Le Roux of the ISS has pointed out that South Africans working in a country that then becomes an area of armed conflict will suddenly find themselves falling foul of the law, and that requiring all South Africans currently working in Iraq to apply for authorisation may cause many of them to return home to minimal employment prospects. Indeed, the complexities of the legislation have already caused Erinys to dismiss its South African employees.[35]

Domestic regulation in the United Kingdom

Regulation of PSCs in the UK has been discussed since at least the late 1990s, but proposals for regulation presented in 2002 have not resulted in legislation. In 1998 the Report of the Sierra Leone Arms Investigation (the 'Legg Report') analysed the Sandline ('arms to Africa') scandal and called for a British government Green Paper into the regulation of private military companies.[36] The Green Paper was published in February 2002 and argues that regulation is necessary because of the practical problems that might be caused by the actions of a British-based military company, such as under-mining British policy. The Green Paper suggests six options for regulation: a ban on military activity abroad; a ban on recruitment for military activity abroad; a licensing regime for military services; a system of regulation and notification; a general licence for companies; and self-regulation, or the crea-tion of a voluntary code of conduct.[37] In August 2002 the House of Commons Foreign Affairs Select Committee responded with the publication of a report, 'Private Military Companies', which recommends that the US model be care-fully examined,[38] that a licensing regime be created requiring disclosure of the company's structures and policies,[39] and that a monitoring and evalua-tion regime be created.[40] In response, the Secretary of State for Foreign and Commonwealth Affairs agreed to look into these recommendations.[41]

However, the UK process has subsequently stalled and it is unclear what will happen next. The industry's rapid growth and the war in Iraq are partly to blame for the slow process, with further delays caused by Cabinet reshuffles. Nevertheless, in March 2005 it was reported that the eventual regulation would be tight because of a recognition that companies 'are taking advantage of unstable political regimes by disregarding humanitarian and ethical codes'.[42]

Changes in the industry and among its key players since 2002 will have complicated the task of keeping potential new regulations up to date. One obvious change is that while the Green Paper responded to the actions of EO and Sandline, these two companies no longer exist and no company in the UK now openly offers the same sort of services.

The UK industry's own views are also in flux. Christopher Beese, chief administrative officer of ArmorGroup, points out that one of his main concerns about regulation was ensuring that the industry distanced itself from the Sandline model. Now that this has happened anyway, the need for regulation is less pressing.[43] Tim Spicer, formerly head of Sandline, is now chief executive officer of Aegis, a PSC that does not sell combat services.

The BAPSC has also been responsible for change in the British regulatory environment. Launched in February 2006, the organisation has already made significant inroads into unifying the position of its 17 members[44] with regard to regulation. Bearpark hopes that the government might give the BAPSC control over UK regulation, in a similar fashion to the way the Bar Council and the General Medical Council regulate barristers and doctors respectively.[45] However, the merits of this type of 'self-regulation' are debatable.

In light of the continuing regulatory debate in the UK, there may be merit in highlighting some of the difficulties associated with each potential type of regulation. The first two options (a ban on military activity abroad and a ban on recruitment for military activity abroad) are the most stringent, but also the most unlikely to be adopted.

In 1976, after British mercenaries were captured and tried for their participation in the civil war in Angola, Prime Minister Harold Wilson ordered an inquiry into the laws that could be used to call the mercenaries to account. Lord Diplock, who led the inquiry, released a report that thoroughly dismissed the idea that legislation could be used to ban foreign military service or to ban the recruitment for such service on UK soil. The Diplock Report argues that a ban on mercenary activity would violate an individual's right to freedom of movement, a right considered part of customary international law.[46] This conflict between bans on mercenary activity and individual freedom of movement has been an international concern since the early twentieth century. During the debate leading to the creation of the Hague Conventions of 1907, designed to codify laws and customs of war on land, an attempt to ban mercenaries outright failed because of concerns about violating freedom of movement. The prohibition of military service on behalf of other states was considered an 'innovation', which 'departed from established usage up to the present time and seriously threatened individual liberty'.[47] Such proposed bans also suffer from serious problems of enforceability: it is difficult to stop individuals leaving the country on a pretext and then undertaking paid military work.[48] As Kinsey points out, it is also plausible that in some cases an outright ban would prevent the sale of useful services, either quasi-humanitarian services like land-mine clearance, or military assistance to weak but legitimate states.[49] The legal and enforcement difficulties associated with banning foreign military service make the first two options inherently unlikely. Moreover, since 2002, the war in Iraq has created a significant and lucrative market for the sale of security services and this sale supports UK policy in Iraq. Both these factors make a ban on either recruitment or service even more unlikely.

The remaining four options are genuinely regulatory, in that they seek to establish procedures for the use of private companies rather than setting out to ban them. A licensing regime would require the government to decide on which activities ought to be allowed and then to create a procedure whereby companies would apply for a licence. Under a regulation and notification scheme, companies would register with the government. Once approved, companies could take up any contract so long as they notified the government of their intentions. Under a general licensing scheme, companies would receive licences specifying the type of work they are allowed to do and the countries where they are allowed to do it. A voluntary code of conduct leaves regulation up to the industry itself.

Other types of domestic regulation

As well as the approaches taken in the US, South Africa and the UK, there are a number of general legal instruments that governments could use to regulate private security industries.

Foreign enlistment legislation

One of the most common pieces of legislation discussed in the literature on the regulation of PSCs is a law designed to prevent the enlistment of soldiers in foreign armies or the recruitment of soldiers for foreign armies on domestic soil (in other words, instruments of the type dismissed by the Diplock Report as violating freedom of movement).[50] However, these instruments are not really relevant for the regulation of today's private security industry. These foreign-enlistment acts were all created in the nineteenth century. By 1898, virtually all states in the international system had some sort of legislation regarding recruitment for or enlistment in foreign militaries.[51] Apart from violating the entrenched customary right under international law to freedom of movement, they are notoriously unenforceable. The large number of Americans who enlisted abroad as volunteers during the First World War drove a significant hole in the legislation, as they were not prosecuted.[52] The movement of foreign volunteers to enlist during the Spanish Civil War presented another challenge. No one has ever been prosecuted for such offences under UK law.[53] Given that these venerable instruments have seldom been used successfully, it is hard to see how they might form the foundation for any future regulation.

The Security Industry Authority (SIA)

In the UK context, authors often suggest that the type of regulation offered for domestic security services under the auspices of the SIA could be applied internationally.[54] Elke Krahmann of Bristol University argues that across the EU domestic regulation should ensure 'that any private security company registered in one of the EU member states, even if hired for personal or site protection in countries such as Iraq, will have been required to go through a substantial vetting process'.[55] The SIA regulates the domestic private security industry, including security guards and door supervisors, and also the sale of security services, like home burglar alarms. It does not currently apply to the international private security industry and officials at the SIA point out that as it is presently constituted it could not be so applied.[56] Not yet active throughout the entire United Kingdom (not yet having extended its ambit to Northern Ireland), the SIA lacks the capacity for the kind of extraterritorial supervision required for the international private security industry.

While the roles of the domestic and international industries are similar in some respects, they are markedly different in others. Whereas private security guards working in the UK are unarmed, PSC employees working abroad are often armed, meaning that each group requires a different level of regulation. Moreover, if a door supervisor goes on a rampage it will affect only his own reputation and perhaps the reputation of his employer. But if there is a disaster involving PSC employees in Iraq or Afghanistan it could have negative ramifications for UK foreign policy. Background checks and licensing can only be a useful tool when accompanied by stringent oversight, which the SIA would not be able to apply internationally. Even if SIA vetting did apply to employees of PSCs, there would be no guarantee that 'bad apples' would be weeded out. No vetting system can predict with complete accuracy whether or not a person without a criminal record will commit a crime in the future. Licensing systems must be accompanied by oversight and enforcement mechanisms to be effective. Finally, because of these problems with the SIA model, neither the SIA, PSC representatives nor the BAPSC favour the extension of SIA's role to regulate the UK element of the international private security industry.[57]

Application of similar legislation

Another way that governments could regulate PSCs is through the application of existing legislation designed to deal with other issues. Just as the United States has adapted its rules regarding the sale of arms abroad, other states could use arms sales regulations to deal with the sale of security services. Krahmann suggests that the private security industry is not as unregulated as it first appears, given that the industry is subject to European mechanisms on armaments and arms exports.[58] However, the instruments she examines are mechanisms designed to deal with the technology associated with weapons of mass destruction and services associated with these weapons, meaning that they do not apply to mainstream PSCs. Clive Walker and Dave Whyte argue that the UK Export Control Act 2002 and the Terrorism Act's provisions about weapons training could be used to regulate PSCs.[59] However, neither of these instruments directly applies to the private security industry. The Terrorism Act covers weapons training only when given to 'terrorists'. Using legislation designed to control trafficking in weapons of mass destruction and training terrorists to control PSCs is redundant; if the activity is already illegal then it makes no difference whether or not the person trafficking or training is employed by a PSC. Moreover, general arms export legislation, as is the case in the United States, often does not have stringent enough oversight mechanisms to supervise a large number of individuals operating in numerous international locations.

General disadvantages of domestic regulation

In many ways, domestic regulation is the most important strand of the web necessary to control the private security industry: because states have traditionally held a monopoly over the use of force, they ought to determine whether and in what ways security services can be sold. In other ways, however, domestic regulation is the weakest strand. The transnational nature of PSCs makes any kind of domestic regulation difficult. There are three specific problems with any domestic approach to regulation.

Extraterritoriality

The most significant obstacle for domestic regulation of the private security industry is the problem of extraterritoriality. The home state (where the PSC is based) is, in effect, regulating an industry that does the vast majority of its business in the territory of other states. The home government may not be the PSC's main employer and so will not necessarily retain any kind of contractual control. Therefore, for domestic regulation to work, it would have to be designed to give the state extraterritorial jurisdiction. More simply put, the state would have to be able to oversee activities abroad and, if necessary, prosecute infractions that occurred in another state. Both extraterritorial oversight and, to an even greater extent, extraterritorial prosecution pose significant difficulties for governments.

Extraterritorial measures are expensive. Supervising a company's operations abroad requires facilities and manpower to ensure substantive oversight. Prosecuting a company or its employees for activities undertaken abroad is even more complex.[60] There are difficulties in securing witness statements and with transporting evidence. In states where prosecutors are elected, such as the United States, a prosecutor must justify why he or she is spending public funds on conducting an unusually expensive trial for an infraction committed abroad, as opposed to focusing limited funds on crimes committed within their usual jurisdiction.

Extraterritorial enforcement has already proved to be a serious issue in both the United States and in South Africa. In the United States, despite legislation designed to enable prosecution of contractors for criminal acts committed abroad, no such prosecutions have occurred. In South Africa, the attempt to design legislation applicable abroad has resulted in questions being asked about which situations fall under the legislation.

Extraterritorial oversight is especially important for the private security industry, given its tendency to operate in weak or failed states with limited judicial capacity. States hosting PSCs may simply be unable to oversee PSC actions or to prosecute transgressors, and contracts may be unenforceable in post-conflict settings.[61] In some cases, contractors are rendered immune from prosecution. To make matters worse, the host state may not have influence over who is allowed to contract for private services;[62] private companies, NGOs and intervening states may all hire whatever private protection they see fit, even if doing so is bad for the host state.

Extraterritorial provisions in domestic legislation to deal with contracts between PSCs and other non-state actors (NGOs and private companies) are also necessary to ensure good behaviour in states with weak judicial systems. Provisions for extraterritorial prosecution in the state sending the PSC can thus protect the state in which the PSC operates, as can robust international law. Relying on domestic regulation to deal with the private security industry does not recognise the difficulties caused by an industry which operates in weak states without the capacity for effective domestic regulation.

There are very few industries that operate in a fashion analogous to PSCs, which conduct their business almost exclusively overseas and are subject only to the regulation of their home state. The analogy between PSCs and container ships is probably closer. Ships need only be registered and meet the regulation of one state in order to operate around the world. Civil aviation provides an interesting counterpoint. Domestic airlines, which are based at home but, of course, operate around the world, are subject to the regulation of the International Civil Aviation Authority, as well as to the rules of their home state. In addition, there are a number of international treaties regarding how problems associated with air travel ought to be solved, ranging from small ones (statutory rights if a flight is delayed) to major ones (how to handle hijacking). Aviation is controlled both domestically and internationally, thus helping to overcome the problems associated with the extraterritorial application of the law.

The balancing act of domestic regulation

Any framework aimed at regulating PSCs domestically must tread carefully, balancing between being so tight that it makes companies less competitive and forces them to seek new bases, and so loose that it hardly makes a difference. The impact of regulation on competitiveness is an issue of concern for PSCs.[63] A licensing regime that were to scrutinise every contract could hinder the ability of companies to deploy quickly, or to deploy at all.[64] However, 'registration and notification' systems might give companies too much free rein. Unless there are serious consequences associated with being removed from the list of approved companies, and unless there are oversight mechanisms to ensure that companies who break the rules will face consequences, registration and notification systems will be prone to abuse.

Extremely tight regulation runs the risk of alienating potential partners for governments, or, even worse, driving them offshore. Governments may well find it useful in the future to be able to rely on PSCs and the risk of prohibitive regulation is that they will deny themselves this option. It is for this reason that it is most unlikely that states such as the US and the UK will opt for outright bans on PSCs. This problem is visible in the shipping industry, where operators who wish to avoid meeting stringent regulations simply register their ships in a state with lax rules. The only likely solution to this problem is to have clear and applicable international standards, as well as domestic rules, meaning that moving offshore would not necessarily mean moving away from oversight.

Regulation of the willing

Regulation may serve to make the more legitimate PSCs even more legitimate, while marginalising their less legitimate competitors. Regulation will have very little effect on the most dangerous elements of the industry. Implementing the proposals set out in the UK Green Paper would not have prevented Simon Mann's coup attempt in Equatorial Guinea. Any new regulation will only serve to control those companies who already want to be controlled. Domestic regulation cannot control or punish those companies or individuals who work for illegitimate or dangerous causes abroad. It would be naive to think that regulating PSCs will solve the problems caused by private actors using force for their own interests around the world. At its best, all regulation (as opposed to a ban) will be able to do is to draw a sharp distinction between the good, the bad and the ugly, and ensure that state contracts only go to legitimate companies. However, the only way to gain control over those entities unwilling to join trade organisations or to apply for governmental licences is to focus on regulation at the international level.

Hard questions need to be asked about domestic regulation. As Lucia Zedner of the University of Oxford argues in relation to the domestic private security industry, reducing security to the level of a commodity to be bought and sold like any other 'denies it any larger ethical purpose … instead of debating what security is for, for whom it must be secured, and by what means, the emphasis of governmental regulation is upon ensuring the health and profitability of the industry'.[65] Ethical concerns about privatising a core function of the state have a long lineage and ought to be considered in any type of regulation.[66] These concerns not only include questions about the nature of security, but also questions about whether privatising security reduces popular control over the decision to use force and whether it is acceptable to fight for profit. While it is not useful to argue that the clock should be turned back and that the reality of today's industry be ignored, it is worth discussing the way the industry should be developed, and to do so demands that ethical questions be confronted.

Conclusion

Examining the state of domestic regulation in the United States, South Africa and the United Kingdom, and discussing the challenges of regulating private security at the domestic level, reveals that while domestic regulation is a good start, by no means does it offer a complete solution to the challenges posed by PSCs. The question remains: what would it take to overcome the problems of domestic regulation? And furthermore, what would a system with fair competition for contracts, deep scrutiny of each licence granted to a PSC, stringent oversight of the performance of that PSC, and clear and organised mechanisms for prosecution for any crimes committed look like? How much work would it take to create the kind of oversight and accountability mechanisms needed, and to ensure the whole system were transparent?

Creating a series of mechanisms to ensure transparency, accountability and oversight is, in a sense, duplicating the procedures in place for state militaries in modern democracies. The decision to use force in a democracy is subject to debate by elected bodies. After the military is sent to fight, its actions are scrutinised by the media and by elected officials. Militaries in modern democracies have a clear and well-recognised system of courts martial, which ensures that transgressors are accountable for their actions. Private security companies operate without democratic debate, without formal oversight and without mechanisms for legal accountability. Moreover, domestic regulation is ill-suited for dealing with an industry that not only operates offshore, but tends to operate in places where the rule of law is hampered. Many of the obstacles for effective domestic regulation might be improved by robust international regulation. It makes sense that an industry that operates internationally should be regulated internationally.

CHAPTER THREE

International Regulation

International law has the potential to be the most effective tool with which to regulate the private security industry. But while the domestic arena suffers from an inevitably limited scope as a potential regulator of PSCs operating internationally and from deficiencies in certain state regulatory models, if there is a regulatory vacuum regarding PSCs, it exists under current international law. International regulation of PSCs would thus demand the formulation of a new legal framework.

There are no specific international laws regarding PSCs and, moreover, the status of PSCs under international humanitarian law (IHL) is unclear. The focus here is on why international law, which is mainly designed to deal with mercenaries, does not currently apply to PSCs, and on the relationship between IHL and the private security industry. An international law approach to PSCs is necessary, but will only work if it treats mercenaries and PSCs as separate rather than like entities.

Existing international law specific to private force

There are three main international legal instruments devised to deal with mercenaries, but none of these apply to today's private security industry.

The Organisation for African Unity (OAU; now the African Union) created an anti-mercenary convention in 1977. The Convention of the OAU for the Elimination of Mercenarism in Africa, which entered into force in 1985, defines mercenaries as 'anyone who, not a national of the State against which his actions are directed, is employed, enrolls, or links himself willingly to a person, group, or organisation … which seeks political destabilization'.[1] This convention considers mercenaries only in the context of their use in overthrowing governments or subverting national liberation movements and is only binding on African states; on both these grounds it is difficult to see how the convention could be used to deal with PSCs, which have wider roles and are ubiquitous.

Article 47 of Protocol I additional to the Geneva Conventions (1977) defines the term 'mercenary' and denies any captured mercenary combatant and prisoner of war status. Article 47 states in full:

1. A mercenary shall not have the right to be a combatant or a prisoner of war.
2. A mercenary is any person who:
(a) is specially recruited locally or abroad in order to fight in an armed conflict;
(b) does, in fact, take a direct part in the hostilities;
(c) is motivated to take part in the hostilities essentially by the desire for private gain and, in fact, is promised, by or on behalf of a Party to the conflict, material compensation substantially in excess of that promised or paid to combatants of similar ranks and functions in the armed forces of that Party;
(d) is neither a national of a Party to the conflict nor a resident of territory controlled by a Party to the conflict;
(e) is not a member of the armed forces of a Party to the conflict; and
(f) has not been sent by a State which is not a Party to the conflict on official duty as a member of its armed forces.

Article 47 is notoriously flawed, containing a large number of loopholes that in practice make it impossible to apply it to mercenaries. The definition it provides is so weak that is has become commonplace to note that 'any mercenary who cannot exclude himself from this definition deserves to be shot – and his lawyer with him!'[2] It contains several key flaws. First, paragraph 2(e), which states that a mercenary must not be a member of the armed forces of a party to the conflict, is easily avoided. All mercenaries need to do is to enroll in the military that hires them. EO and Sandline both ensured that their employees were formally incorporated into the armed forces of their clients.[3]

Second, paragraph 2(c), which argues that a mercenary is motivated by financial gain, as evidenced by noticeably higher pay for the mercenary than for a state soldier, is faulty on two counts. Proving that a mercenary is financially motivated is itself complicated.[4] The Diplock Report concludes that any definition of a mercenary relying on positive proof of motivation would 'either be unworkable or so haphazard in its application as between comparable individuals as to be unacceptable'.[5] Moreover, the requirement in paragraph 2(c) of proof that a mercenary is paid more than a comparable soldier creates another loophole: all mercenaries would need to do to avoid this clause is to ensure that they are paid (at least on paper) exactly the same amount as other soldiers in the same armed force.[6]

Of course, PSCs could also take advantage of these two loopholes, making it unlikely that the law could apply to them. However, there are several more reasons why Article 47 clearly does not apply to PSCs. Paragraph 2(b) indicates that mercenaries actually take part in hostilities; as we have seen, PSCs argue that they do not engage in combat. The *travaux préparatoires* clearly indicate that this paragraph was designed to exclude foreign trainers and advisors from the definition of a mercenary. A good proportion of PSC business falls into this category and would be excluded.[7] Finally, paragraph 2(d) stipulates that mercenaries cannot be nationals of a party to the conflict. This means that American or British nationals working for PSCs but hired by their own states would fall outside the parameters of Article 47.[8]

The United Nations International Convention against the Recruitment, Use, Financing, and Training of Mercenaries was created in 1989 and entered into force in 2001. The convention states that a mercenary is any person who:

- Is specially recruited locally or abroad in order to fight in an armed conflict;
- Is motivated to take part in hostilities essentially by the desire for private gain and, in fact, is promised, by or on behalf of a party to the conflict, material compensation substantially in excess of that promised or paid to combatants of similar rank and functions in the armed forces of that party;
- Is neither a national of a party to the conflict nor a resident of a territory controlled by a party to the conflict; and
- Has not been sent by a State which is not a party to the conflict on official duty as a member of its armed forces.

This definition very closely follows that of Article 47. In a second section the convention expands the definition to include mercenary activity outside armed conflict, including overthrowing and undermining states.[9]

It contains all the loopholes of Article 47 and, for the same reasons, could not be applied to PSCs.

The corpus of international law designed to deal with mercenaries is not only inherently flawed, but clearly cannot be applied to PSCs. The United Nations has indicated that international law on mercenaries needs to be redrafted. Since the 1980s, the UN has enlisted a special rapporteur to examine mercenary activity. There have been two holders of the post: Enrique Bernales Ballesteros, from 1987 until 2004, and Shaista Shameem, from 2004 to 2005. In 2005 the office of the special rapporteur was replaced by a UN Working Group on Mercenaries. Both the special rapporteur and the working group have considered PSCs and mercenaries to be similar entities.[10] But while both special rapporteurs argued for the creation of a new law in light of the development of the private security industry,[11] the working group has called for the ratification of the UN Convention, which, given the convention's inherent problems and inapplicability to today's PSCs, is almost certainly a step backwards.[12]

Mercenaries and PSCs may share similarities in that they both exchange military services for financial gain. However, they provide different services, requiring different levels of oversight. Mercenaries seeking to overthrow governments or to intervene and prolong civil wars require a different level of regulation from PSCs providing security guards, interrogation and land-mine clearance. Moreover, mercenaries pose a particular threat to African states. In 2005, the UN Security Council recognised 'the linkage between the illegal exploitation of natural resources such as diamonds and timber, illicit trade in such resources, and the proliferation and trafficking of arms and the recruitment and use of mercenaries as one of the sources fuelling and exacerbating conflicts in West Africa, particularly in Liberia'.[13] Security Council Resolution 1467 (2003) explicitly argues that the proliferation of small arms and mercenary activity is a threat to West Africa. PSCs do not pose this sort of direct threat because of the services they offer.[14]

Mercenaries and PSCs also differ in their willingness to be regulated. Mercenaries operate outside the boundaries of the law, offering services that are frequently illegal. They do not form trade associations and they do not lobby the government for regulation. PSCs, on the other hand, are advocates of regulation and operate either with explicit government consent (as in the United States) or through an informal system of notifying the government (as is frequently the case in the UK).

It is, of course, true that PSCs provide dangerous services that can influence the outcome of conflicts, and it is clear that these services are currently under-regulated. A useful analogy is the different regulations applying to legal and illegal drugs. All drugs have the potential to be fatal. Pharmaceutical companies that operate openly and work with governments may not be perfectly moral organisations. But trying to control them by using the laws that deal with the sale of illicit street drugs would be impossible. Drug dealers are not concerned about the chemical composition of their products, the welfare of their clients and whether or not they are operating outside the law; they are often closely tied to other criminal organisations. Likewise, mercenaries sell their illegal services regardless of whether or not they might be damaging to their clients, and they are affiliated with and financed by other actors of dubious legal status. The criminal law used to deal with drug dealers could not be applied to pharmaceutical companies, and any legal regime seeking to outlaw mercenaries should not be applied to PSCs.

Both PSCs and pharmaceutical companies have the potential to cause harm. Furthermore, they can both be accused of acting out of concern for profits rather than altruism. Private security companies and pharmaceutical companies have the potential to become dangerous rogue agents, dispensing illegal products or providing services they are not supposed to provide. The solution to the problems potentially caused by pharmaceutical companies is to regulate them tightly, and to ensure that their products and services are frequently tested and held to high standards. The sale of pharmaceutical products is licensed and observed. It is not a perfect system; pharmaceutical companies make mistakes and governments are often accused of working too closely with them. However, it is a good way to control a dangerous service that, without such controls, would exist anyway. PSCs could be controlled in a similar way.

Private security companies and international humanitarian law

There is an interesting relationship between IHL and PSCs. International humanitarian law is both a tool of potential control over PSCs and a further regulatory lacuna. Private security companies are required, like other actors, to abide by the rules set down by IHL on the battlefield. However, confusion remains over the legal status of PSCs under the same set of laws.

International humanitarian law as a source of control

International humanitarian law is composed of the rules of conduct on the battlefield, or what is often called the *jus in bello*. The Geneva Conventions (1949) and the Protocols Additional to the Geneva Conventions (1977) are the key documents of IHL, and set out rules applying to all participants on the battlefield. These rules include elements such as the protection of non-combatants, the rights of prisoners of war and the types of weapons considered legitimate. The International Committee of the Red Cross (ICRC) is at pains to point out that PSCs are not totally unregulated, as they must follow these rules in the same way as all other fighters.[15] International humanitarian law thus guarantees that PSCs will follow certain standards on the battlefield. One way to ensure that PSCs abide by IHL is to include its provisions in contracts, or as part of voluntary codes of conduct or the charters of organisations like the IPOA and the BAPSC.[16]

In theory, asserting that PSCs have a duty to abide by IHL should ensure a minimum standard of behaviour. In practice, relying on IHL as a control mechanism is unwise. International humanitarian law is notoriously weak. It is hard to apply even to state militaries, where there are clear chains of command indicating where orders originate. If IHL fails to deal effectively with government forces, where it is possible to sort out who ordered what and when, why should we assume that it could control PSCs, which are not always clearly placed within the chain of command?

Committing war crimes (breaking the cardinal rules of IHL on genocide or torture) could result in the prosecution of individual contractors by the ICC. However, it is unclear whether US contractors (foreign or American) could be prosecuted given the fact that the US has not signed the Rome Statute. Currently, the ICC does not have jurisdiction over corporations, meaning that PSCs themselves could not be charged with crimes or be held responsible for their employees' acts.[17]

Moreover, IHL appears to be increasingly out of date on today's battlefields. Many commentators have noted that the rise in irregular war, involving civilians, terrorists and individuals whose status is simply unclear, strongly challenges an international legal regime centred around states and organised national liberation movements.[18] Private security companies often note that IHL is not a sufficient form of regulation, given that it no longer matches the realities of war.[19]

While asking PSCs to adhere to IHL would unquestionably constitute a useful element in any regulatory regime, it would not be strong enough on its own to regulate PSCs. Moreover, the status of PSCs themselves under IHL is unclear. One of the main reasons for an inclusive approach to the laws of war is that they function best under conditions of reciprocity. For example, one military will abide by the rules governing the treatment of enemy PoWs because doing so makes it more likely that enemy or other countries' armed forces will treat captured personnel as PoWs. If PSCs are not entitled to the protections of the laws of war, they might be less inclined to abide by them themselves.[20]

The status of private security companies under international humanitarian law

International humanitarian law tries to clarify the status of actors involved in war in order to protect non-combatants. Private security companies unquestionably muddy the IHL waters, as they are civilians clearly assisting in the prosecution of wars. The question of status under IHL is important because if PSCs are not considered to be lawful combatants then they run the risk of losing PoW status and other rights under IHL. If PSCs are considered to be combatants, however, then they become legitimate military targets. Clarifying the status of their employees will be of benefit to the companies themselves and to the governments that hire them.

According to the Geneva Conventions, civilians directly participating in hostilities are considered unlawful combatants, or unprivileged belligerents, and have no rights under IHL.[21] The major question facing PSCs, then, is whether or not their employees participate directly in hostilities. Michael Schmitt of the George C. Marshall European Center for Security Studies has argued that the question of whether contractors can somehow get lawful combatant status is a red herring, given that American military doctrine explicitly rules out the possibility. In all circumstances, 'contractor employees cannot lawfully perform military functions and should not be working in scenarios that involve military combat operations where they might be conceived as combatants'.[22]

There are two particularly important and related questions about the international legal status of contractors. First, can contractors be understood to be combatants and, therefore, do they have the right to PoW status? Second, what constitutes taking a 'direct part' in hostilities, which would mean that contractors were not civilians and so possibly unlawful belligerents and certainly legitimate targets?

Do contractors have prisoner-of-war status?

The Third Geneva Convention (Article 4) describes the three categories of group that are considered to be legitimate combatants and, therefore, entitled to PoW status, one of which (spontaneously organised resistance groups) is not relevant to a discussion about the status of PSCs.[23] To be considered lawful combatants, then, PSCs would have to fall into one of two categories. The first is 'members of the armed forces of a Party to the conflict as well as members of militias or volunteer corps forming part of such armed forces'.[24] The second is:

> members of other militias and members of other volunteer corps, including those of organized resistance movements, belonging to a Party to the conflict and operating in or outside their own territory even if this territory is occupied, provided that such militias or volunteer corps, including such organized resistance movements, fulfil the following conditions:
> a) that of being commanded by a person responsible for his subordinates;
> b) that of having a fixed distinctive sign recognisable at a distance;
> c) that of carrying arms openly;
> d) that of conducting their operations in accordance with the laws and customs of war.

It is not clear how PSCs fit into the first category, as they are not usually formally incorporated into state armies, because 'the purpose of hiring such companies is often to avoid the various employer's responsibilities that members of armies and their dependents enjoy'.[25] Schmitt points out that contractors would find it difficult to claim that they are formal members of the armed forces, because they have not joined the armed forces through the normal procedures (enlistment or conscription) and because the state is capable of, when it chooses, enlisting civilians into the armed forces (as it does with reservists).[26] The employees of PSCs could not be considered to be combatants under Article 4.A(1).

Whether or not PSCs meet the lengthier criteria of Article 4.A(2) is less clear. International law scholar Louise Doswald-Beck argues that the history of this article and its predecessors clearly indicates that states wished to grant PoW status to fighters who were not formally authorised by their governments; as a result, 'it is abundantly clear that a PMC [or PSC] is not precluded from falling within this provision because it is not part of the army or does not have a formal authorisation' from the state. PSCs could choose to ensure that they follow the four specific criteria of organisation.[27]

Schmitt disagrees with Doswald-Beck's interpretation. He argues that Article 4.A(1) is designed to deal with *independent* militias, volunteer corps and resistance movements. The 'very independence of such groups distinguishes them from the regular armed forces; private contractors, by contrast, are typically dependent on the armed forces, if only for fiscal survival'. He concludes that contractors 'seldom if ever qualify for combatant status'.[28]

Direct participation in hostilities

If Schmitt's assertion that PSCs rarely qualify for combatant status is correct, then the question of whether or not they participate directly in hostilities becomes much more important. If PSCs are not combatants, and they *do* engage directly in hostilities, then they run the risk of losing PoW status and could be punished for their participation. Schmitt argues that if an act is critical to the direct application of violence against the enemy, it constitutes participation in hostilities; for example, the tactical-level intelligence used for finding a certain target. Thus, contractors performing some military functions are participating in hostilities directly and run the risk of losing their PoW status and facing punishment for their acts.[29]

As the opposing views of Doswald-Beck and Schmitt on the subject of combatant status suggest, IHL is open to a variety of interpretations. The complexity of IHL is precisely the reason it remains only a blunt instrument with which to regulate the behaviour of PSCs and to ensure their safety on the battlefield. In a situation where decision-making is obscured by the fog of war, it is even more likely that the answers to these questions will either be more unclear or even irrelevant. Even though the consequences for contractors might be significant, it is hard to imagine that fear of losing PoW status would prevent contractors from working for governments or prevent governments from hiring contractors. Given that it is unlikely that any soldier fighting for the 'coalition of the willing' in Iraq will be assured of his Geneva rights, it is difficult to see how the loss of PoW status really matters.

International humanitarian law, because of its complexity and its increasing remove from the reality of war, can neither be relied upon to control PSCs and their employees nor to protect their PoW rights. There are no easy solutions to this problem. Claims that IHL is out of date and that it no longer corresponds to reality are commonplace, as noted above, but it is difficult to see how new rules could be devised in the near future; pursuing change in IHL as a means of regulating the private security industry is likely to be a blind alley.

Problems with international regulation of private security companies

The first and most obvious problem with regulation of PSCs at the international level is that no such specific and effective mechanism for regulation exists. To make matters worse, approaching mercenaries and PSCs as two sides of the same coin and regulating them accordingly ignores the very different problems that each poses. Consequently, the most important step the international community can take to improve regulation of the private security industry is to separate the two issues.

Treating mercenaries and PSCs separately would improve the regulatory prospects for both actors. First, many of the problems associated with the law governing mercenaries stem from the fact that states were trying to exclude many actors whom they did not consider to be mercenaries (like trainers, advisers and national soldiers) from the law.[30] If a different type of law existed for non-combatant trainers and advisers, this loophole could be closed.

Second, some critics argue that states have created weak anti-mercenary law in order to preserve the right to use private military assistance for themselves.[31] If this is true,[32] then creating regulation that legitimises the private security industry will provide states with a legal alternative to hiring private assistance when they need it. States have a right under Article 51 of the United Nations Charter to arrange for their own defence,[33] and regulating the private security industry would allow weak but legitimate states the option of augmenting their forces legally with private assistance.

Third, treating PSCs differently from mercenaries will ensure that the industry itself is engaged in the development of regulation. Industry representatives have indicated that it is unhelpful that the main UN body currently working on the issues posed by private security is called the UN Working Group on Mercenaries.[34] Senior PSC personnel indicate that they do not believe that the working group is a realistic solution to international regulation.[35]

Finally, and most importantly, different regulatory approaches to the issues posed by mercenaries and PSCs will lead to tailor-made law that works to overcome the very different problems posed by each type of actor. It is hard to see how rules affecting the open use of PSCs by states and international organisations could ever be the same as the law required to control the clandestine organisation of illegal acts or the combat support provided to illegitimate rulers.

International humanitarian law could also be better applied to the private security industry. It would be useful for the applicable rules to be clearly summarised and provided to companies themselves. However, senior industry figures indicate that despite asking for such clarification from the ICRC, they have not yet received it.[36]

Improving both the international law regarding mercenaries and IHL will not be easy. A clarification of the status of contractors under IHL is unlikely, given the competing interpretations of the law. The real difficulty with IHL is that it has become out of date; different interpretations result from the fact that those who formulated the law did not envisage the participation of actors like PSCs in battle. Until IHL as a whole is improved, which is extremely unlikely, it is equally unlikely that the status of PSCs will be made crystal clear.

The outlook is less bleak, but far from rosy, for the prospects of improving anti-mercenary law. A change in the law would have to come from the United Nations. Historically, the UN has treated mercenaries and PSCs identically, and appears institutionally hostile towards private force.[37] It would be necessary to obtain a consensus among the relevant parties at the UN, particularly the Working Group on Mercenaries, in order to treat the issues separately and then to develop new types of regulation for each one.

Devising new international law regarding mercenaries and new international regulations would probably prove both time-consuming and expensive. Any international regulation of PSCs would require the creation of an international office to oversee PSC activity. Singer suggests a system of contract review, independent observer teams and some sort of sanctions if violations occur.[38] Setting up such a scheme would be costly, and it would have to be carefully devised in order to ensure that companies already going through a domestic licensing regime do not have to jump through two sets of similar regulatory hoops. If regulatory red tape grows too thick, the necessary support that must come from industry for such system to work would disappear. There would also have to be agreement about the site of the regulatory body: would it be a UN office or an independent agency? As Singer recognises, there is disagreement about the type of sanctions that could be applied to the industry. He suggests that market punishment is insufficient and proposes that the ICC or an ad hoc tribunal, set up for the purpose, could deal with punishments. As has already been noted, the ICC currently has no jurisdiction over corporations and it is unclear how it could apply to American contractors. An ad hoc tribunal is a potential solution, but it could be a costly one. This cost could be met, however, if companies were required to fund the tribunal, either through voluntary contributions or a levy for every licence granted.[39] Ensuring the legitimacy of the tribunal is another problem altogether.

The first step towards more effective regulation would be to treat PSCs and mercenaries differently, which might result in speedier state agreement on new laws and regulations. However, the issues of cost, oversight and the application of sanctions must also be resolved.

Conclusion

Both existing international law and potential regulatory schemes for controlling PSCs are flawed. Existing law is not designed to deal with PSCs; neither the architects of anti-mercenary law nor the formulators of IHL envisaged the participation of PSCs in war. As Dickinson argues, 'it is a perhaps regrettable, but nevertheless true, fact of international law that even state actors are only rarely prosecuted for human-rights abuse. Even if all international instruments were interpreted to apply to private military contractors, we would still need to seek additional alternative accountability mechanisms in order to achieve meaningful oversight.'[40]

Even when the flaws of the existing system have been taken into account, the task of devising any new system is fraught with difficulties. Regulation must be backed by international will and the system must be paid for; it must not duplicate existing domestic regimes unnecessarily. But even though the creation of new regulation might be difficult, it is unquestionably necessary. International regulation has the capacity to protect states with weak judicial systems from potential problems caused by PSCs; it can prevent PSCs from moving abroad to avoid regulation; it can ensure that contracts between non-state actors and PSCs adhere to minimum standards. International law on its own, and as it currently stands, is ineffective as a means of regulating PSCs; with changes, and in tandem with a variety of other approaches, it could serve to ensure that the strengths of the industry are cultivated and its dangerous aspects diminish.

CHAPTER FOUR

Informal Regulation

In addition to the formal domestic and international regulations that apply or could apply to PSCs, it is important to look at the wide range of informal ways through which the private security industry might be regulated. Given that neither domestic nor international regulation offers a complete solution to the regulatory issues posed by PSCs, informal control over the industry has an important role to play. Examining informal regulation on its own highlights an aspect of regulation not normally examined systematically, and demonstrates that informal rules can play a significant part in a wider and more formal regulatory web. While informal regulation is not sufficient in itself, and indeed suffers from a number of problems, it can still complement more official regulation. Five types of informal regulation may have roles to play: the use of the market and reputational pressures; the use of civil actions against contractors; the pressures created by the insurance industry; the use of specifically designed contracts; and collective self-regulation, through industry organisations like the BAPSC and the IPOA.

Reputational pressure and the market

One of the more obvious informal modes of regulating the private security industry is to rely on the market and the desire of companies to preserve their reputations. Companies that are perceived to be or whose employees are found to have been negligent or criminal will not succeed in a competitive marketplace. Accordingly, companies will strive to preserve legitimate reputations that will bring in business.

Reputational pressures and the market have had a clear impact on the shift away from the industry's provision of combat services.[1] There is virtually universal agreement among industry representatives and PSC officials that combat services are simply too controversial to be offered and, as a result, there is no real market for such services.[2] As Dominick Donald puts it, even if British PSCs are requested to provide combat services by the UK government, it 'does not mean that the British PSC sector should, or will, say yes … British PSCs will not in the short to medium term undertake combat tasks because it would wreck their business. The sector has spent too long separating itself from the combat end of the private security spectrum to jeopardise it all with more "dogs of war" headlines'.[3] Indeed, the industry is moving so far away from the combat model that at least one company, Erinys, is considering offering human-rights training as one of its services.[4] Just as combat has disappeared, other services the public finds unacceptable may also disappear.

On its own, however, the market is an imperfect source of regulation. University of Oxford criminologist Lucia Zedner argues, with reference to the domestic private security industry, that markets function best with 'plentiful and accurate' information for consumers, so that they 'know what they have a right to expect or about which sectors they should be wary'.[5]

The absence of effective information is also significant for the international private security market. Cockayne notes that critical non-governmental organisations are hampered in their use of PSCs by a lack of knowledge about the industry, which results in 'significant legal, reputational, operational and strategic risks for those organisations'.[6] Without a more open market, it is difficult for NGOs to make good decisions about when to use PSCs and which PSCs to use.

Relying on market pressures as a form of regulation also assumes that there is only one market for private security services, and that success in that market is undermined by negligence or criminality. In fact, there are two markets for private force: failure in the legitimate market will not necessarily lead to a loss of business overall (although it may lead to the loss of contracts with many high-paying clients). There are parts of the world where a propensity for violating international law might be a unique selling point.[7] The existence of both legitimate and illegitimate markets for private force highlights the fact that there should be two types of international law to regulate them.

The market is also a problematic source of regulation because financial incentives might still persuade firms to take risks and to sacrifice their reputations. The judgement of firms 'may often be influenced by counter-vailing profit motivations. In fact, some firms may decide that going for the 'quick score' is worth the risks of long-term market costs' or they might try to keep lucrative but illicit operations secret.[8]

Civil suits

Another aspect of informal regulation can come from the pursuit of lawsuits against contractors in domestic courts. In the United States, the Alien Tort Claims Act (ATCA) allows non-US citizens to sue in US courts in cases where international law has been violated. There are two lawsuits pending against contractors involved in the Abu Ghraib prison scandal: *Ibrahim vs Titan Corporation* and *Saleh vs Titan Corporation*.

One potential obstacle to the use of civil suits is the legal doctrine known as the 'government contractor' defence, 'which shields government contractors from liability when they build something or provide services in line with government specifications'.[9] A recent decision regarding the case against Titan suggests that the government contractor defence can only apply when contractors are 'acting essentially as soldiers'. As the defendants in the Titan case were not able to prove that they were acting as soldiers, they could not use the defence.[10] Given that there are many other legal reasons, particularly the ramifications for IHL and the rules of US military doctrine outlined in the previous chapter, that contractors cannot claim and would not want to claim to be acting as soldiers, it seems unlikely that contractors will be able to make use of this defence.

A second obstacle to the use of civil suits against contractors under the ATCA is that it must be demonstrated that contractors are acting as representatives of the state, or under the 'color of state law'; given that the contractors at Abu Ghraib 'were acting in close coordination with military personnel at the prison this would seem clear'.[11] However, in the *Ibrahim* and *Saleh* cases, the DC District Court has ruled that the contractors were acting in a purely private capacity and so cannot be held accountable. This decision has been criticised for not recognising the use of the ATCA in other circumstances to deal with private acts.[12]

Another way to allow the use of civil suits is to insist that companies open offices in the countries where they operate, allowing lawsuits to take place in those states. This is not a perfect system, as it presumes an effective judiciary in the home state, but it does open up PSCs to another measure of informal regulation. The requirement to open subsidiary offices abroad could be made either in domestic regulation or through informal collective self-regulation.

Civil suits have potential merit as an additional way to call individual PSC employees to account for their illegal actions, but it is by no means clear that they will always succeed. However, the publicity that such civil suits bring will help to keep problems caused by contractors in the public eye.

Insurance

Zedner points out that insurance can be used to drive regulation because 'the insurance industry is not prepared to offer cover across the private security sector unless recognisable and enforceable standards are instituted upon the basis of which insurers can assess risk and set premiums'.[13] Pressures from insurance companies could force the private security industry to set basic standards for the activities they are prepared to undertake and how their employees are vetted and trained.

In fact, the effects of pressure from the insurance industry are already visible. Some of the potentially more dangerous aspects of the private security business may simply be uninsurable. Beese points out that even if combat operations were possible, insuring them would be very difficult.[14] Thus, any permanent company is unlikely to undertake operations that cannot be insured, and many potential employees will be deterred from working for an employer without insurance. Once again, none of these constraints could apply to groups seeking dubiously legal opportunities.

Contracts

PSCs could also be informally regulated by better-designed contracts, a form of oversight that would not necessarily require any new law. Dickinson argues that contracts could be used to force PSCs to abide by international humanitarian law and human-rights standards; contain specific details about training, performance benchmarks and accreditation; and provide for better monitoring and oversight.[15] The Swiss government and the ICRC embarked on an initiative in 2005 designed to help include IHL standards in industry contracts. Dickinson argues that one of the ways to improve oversight is to add protections for whistleblowers in contracts.[16] ArmorGroup already provides these protections[17] and the IPOA complaints mechanism, discussed below, should serve a similar purpose.

Regulation through contract is also visible in the application of the UN Voluntary Principles on Human Rights, which set out a code of conduct for natural resource and other private companies that contract private security firms and, in situations where the host state government cannot provide security. The Voluntary Principles suggest that:

- PSCs should observe local and humanitarian law;
- PSCs should be technically proficient (especially in the use of fire-arms);
- PSCs should exercise restraint and caution while using force and do so only in accordance with local rules and international guidelines;
- PSCs should have codes of conduct;
- there should be systems in place for investigating allegations of human-rights abuse;
- force should be used only 'preventively and defensively' and avoid activities normally the responsibility of the state military and police;
- companies should check the backgrounds of their employees and exchange information with other companies, states and organisations about these background checks;
- contracts between private companies and private security should include the Voluntary Principles where possible.[18]

Holmqvist correctly points out that the 'conspicuous infrequency with which they [the Voluntary Principles] are mentioned in the literature on private security regulation indicates both that they have so far had a feeble impact'.[19] However, this gap in the literature also reflects the absence of work done on the use of PSCs by other private companies.[20] As the name indicates, the Voluntary Principles are not binding in any sense and could be easily ignored; however, they form an important means of regulating the relationship between PSCs and other non-state actors. The failures of international and domestic law mean that the relationship between private actors and PSCs is noticeably unregulated, and the Voluntary Principles could fill this gap.

Regulation through contract is '*not* a one-size-fits-all approach', meaning that it will be tailored to specific firms and the sale of specific services.[21] Furthermore, regulating PSCs with better contract mechanisms can help to overcome a number of specific problems. Contractually required background checks and oversight mechanisms would go some distance to addressing the problems with domestic regulation. However, the main difficulty with contractual reform is that, unless required by legislation, it would be voluntary. The United States government, for example, is one of the largest clients of private security and uses a flawed contracting system;[22] improving this system would require the US to agree to a change in policy. Neither the Voluntary Principles nor the Swiss government–ICRC project are likely to become binding in the near future. Changing contracts, then, relies on the will of the clients that hire PSCs. The companies themselves are enthusiastic about the idea. Contractual reform has potential for the general enhancement of industry regulation, even if on its own it is insufficient.

Collective self-regulation

The most significant source of informal regulation is collective self-regulation. The IPOA requires its members to sign up to a Voluntary Code of Conduct;[23] it has a permanent committee that hears and investigates complaints from anyone who wishes to lodge them. The BAPSC is a newer organisation and is developing similar mechanisms. The industry is keen on self-regulation for three reasons: first, governments have been slow to create regulation themselves and the industry can fill this gap temporarily.[24] By self-regulating, the industry might be able to influence new governmental regulation: if governments accept industry self-regulation as sufficient, or they rely on industry organisations, or even if new regulation reflects standards already agreed upon in the industry. Second, self-regulation is unlikely to impose overly onerous requirements on member companies. Third, self-regulation increases the industry's legitimacy.

Self-regulation has a number of potential benefits. Industry organisations like the BAPSC and the IPOA can help to distinguish companies that want to operate in a legitimate and above-board fashion (their members) from those companies that do not wish to do so. This would reduce business opportunities for companies that are not members and put pressure on potential clients to hire only those companies that are members. Moreover, industry organisations can have a socialising effect: the desirability of membership in organisations like the BAPSC can help companies that want to develop greater legitimacy to do so. Pressure from fellow members might help to ensure that they continue to avoid illegitimate activities and uphold good human-rights standards. Industry organisations can also apply certain limited sanctions, such as the forfeit of membership privileges for badly behaved members who violate codes of conduct.

Self-regulation also assists transparency. The IPOA and the BAPSC operate websites with promotional materials and information about their members and the industry as a whole. Of course, this information is inherently subjective, but the more public the industry's profile, the more embarrassing potential problems become.

Another advantage of self-regulation is its simplicity. It does not require new legislation, lengthy governmental debates, or the development of international law. Companies can set standards and begin enforcing them rapidly. Both the BAPSC and the IPOA argue that part of the reason they are pursuing self-regulation is not because they believe it to be sufficient on its own, but because of the delays in creating good domestic and international regulation.[25] Any measures that enhance the industry's legitimacy also enhance its business prospects.[26]

Self-regulation does suffer from a number of problems. The most obvious is the accusation of 'foxes minding the chicken coop': the industry, especially given the sensitive nature of the services it provides, might not be its own best monitor. As Singer puts it, 'the incentive structures run against a trade group acting as a strict enforcement and punishment agent for members of its own industry'.[27] Externally imposed rules are likely to be stricter than rules companies decide upon themselves and sanctions more serious.

Effective self-regulation also requires universal membership. Currently, the IPOA and the BAPSC do not encompass all American and British PSCs respectively. The difficulty here is that membership cannot be used as a test of legitimacy, given that major and legitimate players are currently outside the fold. DynCorp is not a member of the IPOA and several companies are still deciding whether to join the BAPSC. Without universal membership, sanctions are fairly meaningless; being expelled from an organisation that already excludes legitimate players will not be as much of a threat as removal from a universal organisation. Moreover, companies failing to meet the standards set can simply resign their membership.[28]

Self-regulation is also problematic because it occurs at the level of companies rather than the level of individuals. The limited sanctions that do apply to the industry apply to the companies, not to their employees. Individual crimes cannot be prevented or dealt with using the mechanisms of industry self-regulation.[29]

Because self-regulation is currently voluntary, it can only ever be as good as PSCs wish it to be. Most companies operating today make a significant effort to be more transparent than in the past and to make sure that their employees are thoroughly vetted and supervised. Depending merely on the goodwill of companies for the long-term oversight of the industry, however, would be risky business.

Improving self-regulation and informal mechanisms

The problems of self-regulation are precisely why no other industry is entirely self-regulated.[30] However, in the UK context, a hybrid system of self-regulation and enabling legislation could resolve the lack of enforcement associated with pure self-regulation, through the creation of a permanent professional organisation with specific powers. The BAPSC and the IPOA could form the nucleus of such an organisation, although a wholly new organisation could be created. To sell security services would require membership in the professional organisation, just as doctors and lawyers must be registered with their professional organisations before practicing, and can lose their licenses if they violate the rules. A professional organisation could insist on minimum training qualifications and specify the kinds of contracts companies are allowed to pursue. Universal membership and the inability to practice without membership would provide significant sanctions and incentives. The success of self-regulation would no longer live and die with the goodwill of the industry's members. Moreover, creating enabling legislation would be politically simpler (both in terms of getting agreement and actual design) than creating a wholly new regulatory regime. The General Medical Council is enabled by the Medical Act of 1858.[31] Legal professional bodies are similarly enabled by legislation.[32] The Bar Council is a particularly interesting analogy. The practice of barristers has always been, in effect, 'self-regulated'; from the fourteenth century, judges governed the profession and in 1894 the Bar Council was formed. In 1987, the Courts and Legal Services Act recognised the Bar Council as the professional body for barristers.[33] Therefore, the precedent for legally enabling an existing professional organisation exists. A group like the BAPSC could be similarly enhanced through legislation.

Improved self-regulation could also help to strike the necessary balance between regulation so stringent it drives companies abroad and regulation so loose that it is meaningless. Legislation could describe the minimum standards that must always be met by the industry and licences could still be required by the government. In effect, the organisation could become a self-enforcing list of approved providers, whose specific contracts would then be supervised by the government. In the UK, the most likely scenario for contract approval would be that contracts for a select group of foreign governments would not be scrutinised; contracts for other states would have to be approved. Combined with effective international legislation to protect weak states and to ensure that PSCs and their employers could be prosecuted, this hybrid system closes many of the gaps that currently exist in the regulation of the private security industry.

The creation of a legally enabled permanent professional organisation could also render market and reputational pressures, as well as government by contract, more effective mechanisms. A loss of reputation might be bad enough for business, but if it is accompanied by tough sanctions from a professional body, including potential exclusion, then the costs are even higher. Part of the function of the professional body could be to require all contracts to contain mechanisms for oversight and basic standards of training.

Self-regulation, even if it is enabled by new legislation to make it stronger, could still face two problems, one that could be easily resolved and one that might prove more difficult. Any industry body that serves the needs of companies like today's main PSCs by nature cannot regulate the kinds of mercenary operations that led to the coup attempt in Equatorial Guinea in 2003. It is unlikely that companies or groups planning illegal activities would ever bother joining such an organisation. It is for this reason that international law dealing specifically with mercenaries is vital.

The second problem is that self-regulation of any kind still leaves the industry in charge of its own oversight. Members of the self-regulating body could fail to enforce the rules effectively, or could change their views on what constitutes a transgression. The legislation establishing these bodies would have to be carefully designed to meet this challenge. Moreover, this sort of body could be combined with more formal domestic regulation requiring a degree of governmental oversight, as well as with international legislation. Improved self-regulation has the capacity to be part of a far more effective regulatory web than the system that currently exists.

CONCLUSION

It may very well be true that, as Singer argues, the cheese industry is better regulated than the private security industry.[1] However, as the discussions of domestic, international and informal regulation reveal, this is in large measure because the cheese industry is nothing like the private security industry.

One of the main reasons why PSCs are so poorly regulated is that they are inherently difficult to regulate. At the domestic level, the problems posed by extraterritorial jurisdiction and the difficulties of creating a licensing regime that strikes a balance between effective measures for oversight, and administration and commercial concerns, make creating regulation challenging. However, domestic regulation alone could never regulate an industry that operates almost entirely abroad.

International regulation of the private security industry runs into a different set of problems. The complexities of defining the industry mean that creating law to govern it will always be challenging. It will be hard to create a legal definition of a PSC that encompasses all of its activities without creating loopholes.

In many ways, however, it seems logical that the best place to regulate an international industry is in the international arena. The major obstacles to international regulation have less to do with its inappropriateness as a venue for regulation and more to do with a lack of agreement on how to proceed and a lack of will to create effective law. The most significant impediment to future international regulation is that the United Nations, the most obvious source of any new international law, persists in treating PSCs and mercenaries in the same way and through the same office. This almost obsessive refusal to recognise reality means that the UN is not an obvious source of future regulation. International rules could be set up, but doing so will require a high level of agreement and the financial ability to make sure that the regulation works.

Setting up blueprints for future regulation is, accordingly, a difficult task. Moreover, different states will have different requirements for regulation, and it may take some time to agree upon specific and effective regulation at the international level. Moves towards regulation of PSCs could involve the following key elements.

Abandon one-size-fits-all approaches to regulation
The international habit of treating all types of private fighters in the same way should end. Treating PSCs and mercenaries identically means that there has not been enough focus on the problems caused by mercenaries and that the reality of the private security industry is not being recognised. International regulation ought to focus only on PSCs and deal with mercenaries separately.

Good oversight mechanisms
Both international and domestic laws dealing with the private security industry are toothless without effective oversight mechanisms. A basic form of oversight can be provided through informal regulation: for example, opening up a clear and easily accessed complaints process, as the IPOA has already done. But formal oversight with serious consequences for transparency is also necessary to ensure that good behaviour does not rely entirely on the continued goodwill of the industry. At the domestic level, oversight can be created through several different mechanisms. First, contracts could be required to spell out the oversight mechanisms that will be used to ensure that they are fulfilled. Second, a domestic licensing body could be given more powers to oversee the industry. In the United States system, this might mean that the ITAR system is complemented by a number of specific observers.

However, effective oversight will require an international element. Companies need to be accountable for their actions wherever they occur and the best way to do so is to create an international body that has the capacity to oversee the industry. Singer's suggestion of the use of tariffs on PSCs to pay for this kind of oversight is potentially useful, but further attention would need to be given to how such a body would be constituted and paid for. An international oversight body is necessary to make sure that PSCs are abiding by IHL (which might not be included in their specific contracts, even though it ought to be) and as a mechanism to allow members of the international public to make complaints.

Improve informal regulation

Informal regulation ought to be encouraged and strengthened along as many lines as possible. There will always be gaps in the web that regulates the private security industry. The combination of domestic and international law will never be perfect; it will always be difficult to find the resources to set up completely effective oversight mechanisms. Properly channelled informal regulation can be used to fill the gaps. The industry's own efforts at self-regulation should be encouraged by legislation that enables them to provide serious sanctions against transgressing members. States should enhance laws like the ATCA and enable civil suits against contractors. Insurance companies can demand higher standards and a clear set of rules about the kinds of jobs PSCs are and are not allowed to take. Contracts need to be carefully drawn and include mechanisms for oversight, and rules about adhering to IHL. Developing informal regulation could help to compensate for the deficiencies of formal regulation. On its own, informal regulation would never be sufficient to deal with an industry as large and as sensitive as the private security industry. Alongside domestic and international regulation, however, it has an important role to play.

Protect weak states

A major goal of any future regulation ought to be the protection of weak states, including those states that use PSCs themselves or states in which PSCs are used. Improving oversight mechanisms and tightening informal regulation will certainly assist with the project of ensuring that PSCs only benefit, rather than detract from, weak states. Treating mercenaries and PSCs as different actors will allow states to use private force themselves if necessary, while diminishing the very real threat still posed by mercenaries.

In addition, two mechanisms would help to protect weak states. First, mechanisms for extraterritorial jurisdiction should be considered in all new domestic regulatory schemes. Extraterritorial jurisdiction affords the possibility of calling PSC employees to account in their home states, if the host state is unable to prosecute. Another related option is for states sending PSCs alongside their own forces to bring PSC employees under the already existing web of military justice.[2]

Second, more attention needs to be paid to the use of private security by private sector entities. PSCs employed by other private actors and operating in weak states are unaccountable, not only because the state's judiciary might not be strong enough to deal with transgressions, but because extraterritorial jurisdiction rules like the MEJA do not apply. The UN's Voluntary Principles are a good start, but they remain elective. One way to ensure that the private sector–private security relationship is regulated is to make sure that international laws apply and to allow for the oversight of these laws.

Make the rules clearer and the industry more transparent

Lack of clarity is a significant problem in the current regulatory environment. It is not clear which rules apply to contractors and when; it is unclear whether and how contractors can be prosecuted. A major goal of new regulation should be to bring greater clarity to the operations of PSCs. The issue of status under IHL needs to be resolved more definitively, while the creation of extraterritorial jurisdiction and new international regulations will help to answer the question of how to prosecute contractors.

New regulation must not make the situation more complex. International regulation must be careful that it does not simply duplicate existing domestic mechanisms.

A more open debate about the future of regulation should also bring much-needed transparency to the private security industry. It is impossible to discuss the regulation of PSCs sensibly if the public does not have access to PSC contracts, and cannot find evidence on how much the industry costs and how many people are employed in it. One of the goals in any regulatory project should be to determine the appropriate level of oversight. Determining how much regulation is too much will help to shape the future of the industry. But without clear information, it will not be possible to do so. One of the goals of regulation should be to make sure that information about the industry is freely available.

A regulatory web: add more strands and fill the gaps

Private security companies do not exist in a regulatory vacuum; rather, they operate within an existing regulatory web, replete with rules but also with gaps. One of the reasons it is important to take informal regulation seriously is so that informal rules can fill these gaps in the regulatory web.

The best way to regulate an industry that is complicated, operates across borders and might just be inherently difficult to regulate is to ensure that regulation occurs on as many levels as possible. Regulation of the private security industry can never be as effective as the regulation of the cheese industry. The improvements outlined above will ensure that the web governing the private security industry is tightened. It adds some new strands, like international regulation specifically oriented towards PSCs. Gaps, like that caused by the absence of extraterritorial prosecution, can likewise be filled in. Designing a perfect system to regulate the private security industry is likely to be impossible; domestic regulation will need to be accompanied by international regulation, and both face obstacles. The next best thing after a perfect system is a complex of overlapping systems, which may be individually imperfect but cover as wide a range of issues as possible. The regulatory web that controls PSCs is currently too loose and too easily circumvented.

PSCs cut to the heart of a number of issues in international relations: the traditional powers of the sovereign state, changes in the nature of war and the future of modern militaries. As a result, the regulation of PSCs will always be difficult. But the very contentiousness of the private security industry demonstrates why regulation is necessary. The activities of PSCs raise big questions about the state, war and public control over the use of force, and regulation can help to answer these questions. Regulation can help to find clarity on a battlefield made more complex as war changes; regulation can assist in determining how far the state should relinquish aspects of its monopoly on force; regulation can help to determine what modern armed forces should look like. The regulation of the private security industry may never resemble the kind of regulation applied to simple domestic industries, but that does not mean that such regulation will be ineffective. A regulatory web is a simple yet fairly elegant solution to a complicated and dangerous problem, and offers the best opportunity to control the private security industry.

NOTES

Introduction

1 Steven J. Zamparelli, 'Contractors on the Battlefield: What Have We Signed Up For?', *Air Force Journal of Logistics*, vol. 23, no. 3, Fall 1999, pp. 6–7.

2 Janice E. Thomson, *Mercenaries, Pirates, and Sovereigns: State-Building and Extraterritorial Violence in Early Modern Europe* (Princeton, NJ: Princeton University Press, 1994).

3 Peter W. Singer, 'War, Profits and the Vacuum of Law: Privatized Military Firms and International Law', *Colombia Journal of Transnational Law*, vol. 42, no. 2, Spring 2004; Fred Schreier and Marina Caparini, *Privatising Security: Law, Practice and Governance of Private Military and Security Companies* (Geneva: Geneva Centre for the Democratic Control of Armed Forces, March 2005), p. 3.

4 Singer, *The Private Military Industry and Iraq: What Have We Learned and Where to Next?* (Geneva: Geneva Centre for the Democratic Control of Armed Forces, November 2004), p. 14.

5 Deborah Avant, *The Market for Force: The Consequences of Privatizing Security* (Cambridge: Cambridge University Press, 2005), p. 234; Singer, *Corporate Warriors: The Rise and Fall of the Privatized Military Industry* (Ithaca, NY: Cornell University Press, 2003), p. 222.

6 Fredrick A. Stein, 'Have We Closed the Barn Door Yet? A Look at the Current Loopholes in the Military Extraterritorial Jurisdiction Act', *Houston Journal of International Law*, vol. 27, no. 3, May 2005, p. 589.

7 Steven L. Schooner, 'Contractor Atrocities at Abu Ghraib: Compromised Accountability in a Streamlined, Outsourced Government', *Stanford Law and Policy Review*, vol. 16, no. 2, 2005, p. 556.

8 Singer, *The Private Military Industry and Iraq*, p. 14.

9 The International Peace Operations Association (http://ipoaonline.org/php/) and the British Association of Private Security Companies (http://www.bapsc.org.uk/).

10 See chapter three for details.

11 House of Commons Foreign Affairs Committee, *Private Military Companies: Options for Regulation* (London: The Stationery Office Ltd, 2002).

Chapter One

1 Avant, *Market for Force*, p. 9.
2 Singer, *The Private Military Industry and Iraq*, p. 3.
3 Avant, *Market for Force*; Singer, *Corporate Warriors*.
4 David Isenberg, *A Fistful of Contractors: The Case for a Pragmatic Assessment of Private Military Companies in Iraq* (London: British American Security Information Council, 2004); Isenberg, *The Good, the Bad, and the Unknown: PMCs in Iraq* (London: British American Security Information Council, 2006).
5 Percy, 'This Gun's for Hire: A New Look at an Old Issue', *International Journal*, vol. 58, no. 4, Autumn 2003; Christopher Kinsey, *Corporate Soldiers and International Security: The Rise of Private Security Companies* (London: Routledge, 2006).
6 Avant, *Market for Force*, p. 20.
7 Ibid., p. 16; Singer, *The Private Military Industry and Iraq*.
8 Avant, 'Think Again: Mercenaries', *Foreign Policy*, no. 143, July/August 2004.
9 Isenberg, *Fistful of Contractors*, p. 21.
10 Robert Young Pelton, *Licensed to Kill: Hired Guns in the War on Terror* (New York: Crown Publishers, 2006), pp. 285–7.
11 Singer, *The Private Military Industry and Iraq*, p. 6.
12 Avant, *Market for Force*, p. 21.
13 Erinys, *The Erinys Iraq Oil Protection Force: Infrastructure Security in a Post-Conflict Environment* (London: Erinys, November 2005).
14 Occasionally larger companies have in-house security expertise.
15 James Cockayne, *Commercial Security in Humanitarian and Post-Conflict Settings: An Exploratory Study* (New York: International Peace Academy, 2006).
16 Avant, *Market for Force*.
17 Steven Brayton, 'Outsourcing War: Mercenaries and the Privatization of Peacekeeping', *Journal of International Affairs*, vol. 55, no. 2, Spring 2002, p. 310; Thomas K. Adams, 'The New Mercenaries and the Privatization of Conflict', *Parameters, US Army War College Quarterly*, vol. 29, no. 2, Summer 1999.
18 Singer, *Corporate Warriors*, p. 91.
19 Kinsey, *Corporate Soldiers and International Security*; Avant, *Market for Force*, pp. 21–22; Caroline Holmqvist, *Private Security Companies: The Case for Regulation* (Stockholm: Stockholm Institute for Peace Research, 2005), pp. 5–6; Elke Krahmann, 'Regulating Private Military Companies: What Role for the EU?', *Contemporary Security Policy*, vol. 26, no. 1, 2005, pp. 106–8.
20 Interview with Christopher Beese, London, 12 September 2006; interview with John Holmes, London, 13 September 2006.
21 Holmqvist, *Private Security Companies*, p. 5.
22 Ibid.; E. Kwakwa, 'The Current Status of Mercenaries in Armed Conflict', *Hastings International and Comparative Law Review*, no. 14, 1990, p. 71.
23 Avant, *Market for Force*, pp. 21–2.
24 Ibid., p. 23.
25 Simon Chesterman and Chia Lehnhardt, eds, *From Mercenaries to Market: The Rise and Regulation of Private Military Companies* (Oxford: Oxford University Press, forthcoming 2007).
26 Singer, *Corporate Warriors*, p. 8.
27 Avant, *Market for Force*, p. 8; see also Krahmann, 'Regulating Private Military Companies', pp. 106–8.
28 Avant, *Market for Force*, p. 45.
29 Ibid., p. 219.
30 Ibid., p. 128.
31 Ibid.
32 Zamparelli, 'Contractors on the Battlefield', p. 8.
33 Singer, *The Private Military Industry and Iraq*, p. 10.
34 Clive Walker and Dave Whyte, 'Contracting out War? Private Military Companies, Law and Regulation in the United Kingdom', *International Comparative Law Quarterly*, vol. 54, no. 3, 2005, p. 666.
35 Avant, 'The Implications of Marketized Security for IR Theory: The Democratic

Peace, Late State Building, and the Nature and Frequency of Conflict', *Perspectives on Politics*, vol. 4, no. 3, September 2006, p. 512.

36 See also Percy, 'Morality and Regulation' in *From Mercenaries to Market*.

37 Singer, *The Private Military Industry and Iraq*, p. 8.

38 Zamparelli, 'Contractors on the Battlefield', p. 18; Holmqvist, *Private Security Companies*, p. 29; Singer, *The Private Military Industry and Iraq*, p. 7.

39 Singer, *The Private Military Industry and Iraq*, p. 8.

40 Schreier and Caparini, *Privatising Security*, p. 48.

41 Isenberg, *Fistful of Contractors*, p. 22.

42 Schreier and Caparini, *Privatising Security*, p. 47.

43 Holmqvist, *Private Security Companies*, p. 26.

44 Singer, *The Private Military Industry and Iraq*, p. 18.

45 Alan Green, 'Early Warning: The U.S. Army Can Hardly Be Surprised by Its Problems with Contractors in Iraq', *Center for Public Integrity*, 4 May 2004.: http://www.publicintegrity.org/report. aspx?aid=274. For the original memo see: http://www.publicintegrity.org/docs/ ArmyMemo1.pdf.

46 Schreier and Caparini, *Privatising Security*, p. 59.

47 *Ibid.*, p. 57.

48 Singer, *The Private Military Industry and Iraq*, p. 12.

49 Geoffrey Best, *Humanity in Warfare: The Modern History of the International Law of Armed Conflicts* (London: Weidenfeld and Nicolson, 1980), p. 60.

50 Chapter four discusses these issues in greater depth.

51 Interview with Andrew Bearpark, London, 12 September 2006; interview with Christopher Beese, London, 12 September 2006; interview with Holmes, London, 12 September 2006.

52 Interview with Bearpark, London, 12 September 2006.

53 Avant, *Market for Force*, p. 222.

54 Holmqvist, *Private Security Companies*, p. 29; Michael N. Schmitt, 'Humanitarian Law and Direct Participation in Hostilities by Private Contractors or Civilian Employees', *Chicago Journal of International Law*, vol. 5, no. 2, 2005, p. 515.

55 Singer, *The Private Military Industry and Iraq*, p. 8.

56 *Ibid.*, p. 4.

57 Avant, 'Fact Sheet: Private Security and Contracting for Military Services in the US', unpublished conference material, American Political Science Association annual meeting, 2006.

58 Schmitt, 'Humanitarian Law', p. 518.

59 Walker and Whyte, 'Contracting out War', p. 651.

60 Schooner, 'Contractor Atrocities'.

61 Avant, 'Think Again', p. 22.

62 Dawn Kopecki, 'When Outsourcing Turns Outrageous: Contractors May Be Saving the Army Money but Fraud Changes the Equation', *Business Week*, 31 July 2006.

63 Holmqvist, *Private Security Companies*, pp. 30–31.

64 Singer, *The Private Military Industry and Iraq*, p. 10.

65 Dickinson, 'Contract as a Tool for Regulating Private Military Companies', in *From Mercenaries to Market*, p. 6.

66 Isenberg, *Fistful of Contractors*, p. 27.

67 Singer, *The Private Military Industry and Iraq*, p. 16.

68 Pratap Chatterjee, 'Defence Base Act Contractor Casualty Report', available at: http://www.mountainrunner.us/files/ contractordeaths1.pdf .

69 Isenberg, *The Good, the Bad and the Unknown*, p. 9.

70 Singer, *The Private Military Industry and Iraq*, p. 17.

71 *Ibid.*; Holmqvist, *Private Security Companies*, p. 31.

72 Tim Reilly, Director of Energy Projects, Erinys, pointed out that this is an important feature of regulation. Interview with author, London, 13 September 2006.

73 Dominick Donald, *After the Bubble: British Private Security Companies after Iraq* (London: Royal United Services Institute, 2006).

Chapter Two

1 Avant, *Market for Force*, p. 149.
2 The text of the ITAR is available at: http://www.pmdtc.org/itar_index.htm.
3 Avant, *Market for Force*, p. 150.
4 *Ibid.*
5 Holmqvist, *Private Security Companies*, p. 51; Singer, 'War, Profits', p. 538; Avant, *Market for Force*, pp. 150–51.
6 Avant, 'Privatizing Military Training', *Foreign Policy in Focus Policy Brief*, vol. 7, no. 6, May 2002.
7 Avant, *Market for Force*, p. 151; Kinsey, *Corporate Soldiers and International Security*, p. 137.
8 Avant, *Market for Force*, p. 151.
9 Singer, 'War, Profits', p. 539.
10 Martha Minow, 'Outsourcing Power: How Privatizing Military Efforts Challenges Accountability, Professionalism, and Democracy', *Boston College Law Review*, vol. 46, no. 5, September 2005, p. 1005.
11 Schooner, 'Contractor Atrocities', p. 560.
12 *Ibid.*, p. 560.
13 Minow, 'Outsourcing Power', p. 1007. The company is Aegis.
14 Schooner, 'Contractor Atrocities', p. 560.
15 *Ibid.*, p. 569.
16 Holmqvist, *Private Security Companies*, p. 31.
17 Schooner, 'Contractor Atrocities', p. 565.
18 Avant, *Market for Force*, 234.
19 The change was made by National Defense Authorization Act for Fiscal Year 2005.
20 Stein, 'Have We Closed the Barn Door Yet?', p. 599.
21 Isenberg, *Fistful of Contractors*, p. 66.
22 Avant, *Market for Force*, p. 234.
23 Stein, 'Have We Closed the Barn Door Yet?', p. 596.
24 *Ibid.*, p. 602.
25 Indeed, as of 2004, there had only been one prosecution of any kind using the MEJA; *Ibid.*, p. 597.
26 Kevin A. O'Brien, 'Military Advisory Groups and African Security: Privatized Peacekeeping?', *International Peacekeeping*, vol. 5, no. 3, Autumn 1998, p. 83.
27 Avant, *Market for Force*, p. 161.
28 South African Regulation of Foreign Military Assistance Act available at: http://www.up.ac.za/publications/gov-acts/1998/act15.pdf.
29 Avant, *Market for Force*, p. 163.
30 Holmqvist, *Private Security Companies*, p. 52.
31 Kinsey, *Corporate Soldiers and International Security*, p. 139.
32 Avant, *Market for Force*, p. 163.
33 *Ibid.*
34 Percy, 'This Gun's for Hire', p. 736.
35 Nathan Hodge, 'Army for Hire: Two New Books on the Global Market for Armed Force', *Slate*, 31 August 2006.
36 Sir Thomas Legg and Sir Robin Ibbs, *Report of the Sierra Leone Arms Investigation* (London: The Stationery Office Ltd, 1998).
37 House of Commons Foreign Affairs Select Committee, *Private Military Companies: Options for Regulation* (London: The Stationery Office Ltd, 2001-2002), pp. 20–21, 22–7: http://www.parliament.the-stationery-office.co.uk/pa/cm200102/cmselect/cmfaff/922/92202.htm.
38 *Ibid.*, p. 11.
39 *Ibid.*, p. 35.
40 House of Commons Foreign Affairs Select Committee, *Private Military Companies: Response of the Secretary of State for Foreign and Commonwealth Affairs* (London: The Stationery Office Ltd, 2001–02), p. 39.
41 *Ibid.*, pp. 5–6.
42 Clayton Hirst, 'Dogs of War to Face New Curbs in Foreign Office Crackdown', *Independent*, 13 March 2005.
43 Interview with Beese.
44 As of September 2006.
45 One difference might be that some professional organisations regulate their members with the assistance of legislation.
46 Lord Diplock, Derek Walker-Smith and Geoffrey de Freitas, *Report of the Committee of Privy Counsellors Appointed to Inquire into the Recruitment of Mercenaries*

('Diplock Report') (London: Stationery Office Ltd, 1976), p. 4.

47 Antonio S. de Bustamente, 'The Hague Convention Concerning the Rights and Duties of Neutral Powers and Persons in Land Warfare', *American Journal of International Law*, vol. 2, no. 1, 1908, p. 100.

48 Diplock Report, p. 4.

49 Kinsey, *Corporate Soldiers and International Security*, p. 141.

50 Kim Richard Nossal, 'Global Governance and National Interests: Regulating Transnational Security Corporations in the Post-Cold War Era', *Melbourne Journal of International Law*, vol. 2, no. 2, October 2001, p. 465; Juan Carlos Zarate, 'The Emergence of a New Dog of War: Private International Security Companies, International Law, and the New World Disorder', *Stanford Journal of International Law* vol. 34, Winter 1998; Kinsey, *Corporate Soldiers and International Security*; Singer, 'War, Profits'.

51 47 states had such legislation. Thomson, *Mercenaries, Pirates, and Sovereigns*, p. 81.

52 P.W. Mourning, 'Leashing the Dogs of War: Outlawing the Recruitment and Use of Mercenaries', *Virginia Journal of International Law*, vol. 22, 1982, p. 597.

53 Nossal, 'Global Governance and National Interests', p. 465.

54 Holmqvist, *Private Security Companies*, p. 54.

55 Krahmann, 'Regulating Private Military Companies', p. 110.

56 Interview with Kaye Law, Director of Strategic Development, SIA, London, 25 September 2006.

57 Interviews with Beese, Bearpark and Holmes.

58 Krahmann, 'Regulating Private Military Companies', pp. 108–10.

59 Walker and Whyte, 'Contracting out War', pp. 656–7.

60 Beese and Holmes both highlighted the challenges posed by extraterritorial jurisdiction. Interview with Beese; interview with Holmes.

61 Cockayne, *Commercial Security*, p. 12.

62 Holmqvist, *Private Security Companies*, p. 14.

63 Interviews with Beese, Bearpark and Holmes.

64 Interview with Dominic Donald, Senior Analyst, Aegis Specialist Risk Management. London, 25 September 2006.

65 Lucia Zedner, 'Liquid Security: Managing the Market for Crime Control', *Criminology and Criminal Justice*, vol. 6, no. 3, 2006, p. 282.

66 Percy, 'Mercenaries: Strong Norm, Weak Law', *International Organization*, forthcoming 2007.; Percy, 'Morality'.

Chapter Three

1 OAU, 'Convention for the Elimination of Mercenarism in Africa': http://www.africa-union.org/Official_documents/Treaties_Conventions_Protocols/Convention_on_Mercenaries.pdf.

2 Originally quoted in Best, *Humanity in Warfare*, p. 375, fn. 83; Françoise Hampson, 'Mercenaries: Diagnosis before Prescription', *Netherlands Yearbook of International Law*, no. 3, 1991, p. 29; David Kassebaum, 'Question of Facts: the Legal Use of Private Security Firms in Bosnia', *Columbia Journal of Transnational Law*, vol. 38, no. 3, 2000; Dino Kritsiotis, 'Mercenaries and the Privatization of Warfare', *Fletcher Forum of World Affairs*, vol. 22, no. 2, Summer/Fall 1998, p. 5; In 'War, Profits', p. 531, fn. 39, Singer notes that a private military industry representative used this phrase 'without any kind

of attribution to another source, indicating that Best's legal lessons have been internalized in the private military industry'.

3   Zarate, 'Emergence', p. 124; Singer, 'War, Profits', p. 532; David Shearer, *Private Armies and Military Intervention*, Adelphi Paper 316 (Oxford: International Institute for Strategic Studies, 1998), p. 18.

4   Kwakwa, 'Current Status', p. 71; H.C. Burmester, 'The Recruitment and Use of Mercenaries in Armed Conflict', *American Journal of International Law*, vol. 72, no. 1, 1978, p. 39.

5   Diplock Report, p. 2.

6   For an extensive discussion of the loopholes in Article 47 and the UN convention and their ramifications, see Percy, 'Mercenaries'.

7   *Ibid.*

8   Kinsey, 'Challenging International Law: A Dilemma of Private Security Companies', *Conflict, Security and Development*, vol. 5, no. 3, 2005, p. 291.

9   UN Convention available at: http://www. icrc.org/ihl.nsf/WebPrint/530-FULL? OpenDocument.

10   See UN Doc A/53/338, p. 7 for Ballesteros's position. Shameem acknowledged that there may be a difference between the two groups, but the title of the UN Working Group on Mercenaries and its application to the private security industry clearly demonstrates how the UN treats both types of private actor in the same way.

11   Shameem reiterated Ballesteros's position on this issue; see UN Doc A/60/263 (2005), p. 17.

12   UN Doc E/CN.4/2006/11/Add.1, p. 11.

13   S/Res/1607 (2005), S/Res/1478 (2003) called upon member states to curb the movement of mercenaries and small arms fuelling the conflict in Liberia.

14   Some critics argue that PSCs still pose a threat to weak states through their relationships with natural resource extraction companies. Angela McIntyre and Taya Weiss, 'Financing "National Security" in Africa: PMCs as Long-Term Stakeholders', in Chesterman and Lehnhardt, eds, *From Mercenaries to Market*.

15   ICRC, 'International humanitarian law and private military/security companies': http://www.icrc.org/web/eng/siteengo. nsf/html/pmc-fac-230506.

16   See chapter four for further details.

17   Kathleen M. Jennings, *Armed Services: Regulating the Private Military Industry*, Fafo Report 532 (Oslo: Fafo, 2006), p. 51.

18   Eric Talbot Jensen, 'Combatant Status: It Is Time for Intermediate Levels of Recognition for Partial Compliance?', *Virginia Journal of International Law*, vol. 46, no. 1, 2005; Rosa Brooks Ehrenreich, 'War Everywhere: Rights, National Security Law, and the Law of Armed Conflict in the Age of Terror', *University of Pennsylvania Law Review*, no. 153, 2004.

19   Individual interviews with Beese and Bearpark, 12 September 2006.

20   This argument has often been made in relation to denying mercenaries PoW status: it is unclear whether or not mercenaries would be willing to treat captured prisoners properly if they had no chance of such treatment themselves. For an example see Kwakwa, 'Current Status', p. 89. While PSCs are not automatically excluded from PoW status in the same way as mercenaries, their status remains unclear.

21   Schmitt, 'Humanitarian Law', p. 520.

22   *Ibid.*, p. 523, fn. 53.

23   Louise Doswald-Beck, 'Private Military Companies under International Humanitarian Law', in Chesterman and Lehnhardt, eds, *From Mercenaries to Market*.

24   Third Geneva Convention, Article 4.A(1): http://www.unhchr.ch/html/menu3/b/91. htm.

25   Doswald-Beck, 'Private Military Companies'.

26   Schmitt, 'Humanitarian Law', p. 524.

27   Doswald-Beck, 'Private Military Companies'.

28   Schmitt, 'Humanitarian Law', p. 531.

29   *Ibid.*, pp. 534–6.

30   Percy, 'Mercenaries: Strong Norm, Weak Law'.

31   Antonio Cassese, 'Mercenaries: Lawful Combatants or War Criminals?', *Zeitschrift*

für ausländisches öffentliches Recht und Völkerrecht, vol. 40, 1980, p. 11. The same argument is made in relation to the OAU Convention by James Larry Taulbee, 'Myths, Mercenaries and Contemporary International Law', *California Western International Law Journal*, vol. 15, 1985, p. 347; Zarate, 'Emergence', p. 129; Singer, 'War, Profits', p. 529.

32 I am not convinced this interpretation is correct. See Percy, 'Mercenaries: Strong Norm, Weak Law'.

33 Singer, 'War, Profits', p. 544.

34 UN Doc A/60/263, p. 21.

35 Interviews with industry representatives, September and October 2006.

36 Interviews with officials, 2006.

37 Percy, 'UN Security Council'; Percy, 'Morality'.

38 Singer, 'War, Profits', p. 546.

39 *Ibid.*, p. 543.

40 Dickinson, 'Contract as a Tool for Regulating Private Military Companies', p. 34.

Chapter Four

1 Percy, 'Mercenaries: Strong Norm, Weak Law'.

2 Interviews with Bearpark, Holmes, Doug Brooks, IPOA, Donald and Beese. Interview with Tim Spicer, 11 September 2003. The exception may prove to be Blackwater.

3 Donald, *After the Bubble*, p. 36.

4 Interview with Holmes.

5 Zedner, 'Liquid Security', p. 275.

6 Cockayne, *Commercial Security*, p. 2.

7 Singer makes a similar point. Singer, *Corporate Warriors*, p. 219.

8 *Ibid.*, p. 224.

9 Isenberg, *Fistful of Contractors*, p. 63.

10 *Ibrahim vs. Titan Corp.* For an excellent discussion of these issues, see the unpublished thesis of Tessa Khan, 'The Legal Accountability of Private Military Contractors', University of Western Australia, 2006.

11 Isenberg, *Fistful of Contractors*, p. 64.

12 Khan thesis.

13 Zedner, 'Liquid Security', p. 276.

14 Interview with Beese.

15 Dickinson, 'Contract as a Tool for Regulating Private Military Companies'.

16 *Ibid.*

17 Interview with Beese.

18 The Voluntary Principles on Security and Human Rights: http://www.voluntaryprinciples.org/principles/private.php.

19 Holmqvist, *Private Security Companies*, p. 48.

20 Avant makes the only thorough examination of these relationships in the current literature and the bulk of her analysis is about the use of private security by an NGO: Avant, *Market for Force*, ch. 5.

21 Dickinson, 'Contract as a Tool for Regulating Private Military Companies'.

22 See chapter two and Schooner, 'Contractor Atrocities'.

23 IPOA code of conduct: http://ipoaonline.org/en/standards/code.htm.

24 Interview with Bearpark.

25 Interview with Brooks, 27 September 2006; interview with Bearpark, 19 September 2006.

26 Interview with Brooks.

27 Singer, 'War, Profits', p. 543.

28 Zedner, 'Liquid Security', p. 274.

29 Singer, *The Private Military Industry and Iraq*.

30 *Ibid.*

31 The legislation of the General Medical Council is available from: http://www.gmc-uk.org/about/legislation/index.asp.

32 The Law Society relies on the Solicitors Act 1974.

[33] For the Courts and Legal Services Act, see: http://www.opsi.gov.uk/ACTS/acts1990/Ukpga_19900041_en_1.htm. The UK government is proposing the creation of a new law governing all legal services, the Legal Services Bill: http://www.official-documents.co.uk/document/cm68/6839/6839.asp.

Conclusion

[1] See introduction.
[2] Interview with Donald.